A *Poets & Writers'* Best
Nonfiction Debut
A Barnes & Noble Discover
Great Writers Pick

'Explores the intricacies of the human psyche with stunning poignancy.'
Newsweek, Editor's Choice

'This powerful, haunting memoir starts off with one of the more compelling first sentences I've read in some time: "The night before he died, I promised my dad I would write a book for him." … a journey that takes Vanasco into the dark depths of her family history, as well as her own psyche, and it shows in an incredibly intimate way the methods we use to cope with loss, disappointment, and grief, and how we can try and make our way out of the darkness and into a place of recovery.'
NYLON, Editor's Choice

'Wildly innovative.'
New York Magazine

'Hypnotic… a haunting exploration of perception, memory, and the complexities of grief. In language that is understated and eco-nomical, Vanasco brings to life the father she loved with an almost frightening force… Vanasco's characters and settings are vivid, prismatic, and surreal.'
The New York Times Book Review

'Jeannie Vanasco explores this link between mental illness and the compulsion to write in her new memoir… we soon come to understand that she could not *not* write this book.'
LA Review of Books

'Jeannie Vanasco has crafted a book that will worm its way under your skin, a book that will not give you easy answers or heartwarming takeaways much in the same way that life will not give you easy answers or heartwarming takeaways. Jeannie Vanasco has created a book that I cannot stop thinking about.'
Emily Ballaine, Green Apple Books

'A deceptively s⸺ ⸺ sudden
fecundity and

Kirkus

'Powerful and ruminative… This is an illuminating manual for understanding grief and the strange places it leads.'

Publishers Weekly

'An intense and unforgettable memoir, as fascinating for its artistry as for its subject matter. Lyric, haunted, smart and tortured, this is an obsessive love letter to a dead father as well as a singular work of literature.'

Shelf Awareness

'Vanasco's candor, curiosity, and commitment to human understan-ding are not to be missed.'

Booklist, Starred Review

'Brilliant… As the pages fly by, we're right by Vanasco, breathlessly experiencing her grief, mania, revelations, and – ultimately - relief.'

Entertainment Weekly

'Vanasco's deeply intimate story of loss, grief, and mental illness reads as though it happened just last week, yesterday, today. There's a particular "nowness" to it: an in-the-moment immediacy that plants readers directly into Vanasco's experience.'

Bustle

'Vanasco is brilliant, and this book proves it.'

Darin Strauss, author of *Half a Life*

'A piece of truth so bright it might be your own broken heart handed back to you.'

Melissa Febos, author of *Abandon Me*

'What begins as an experience of profound loss becomes an obsess-sion, the fierce intensity of which propels readers through this breathtaking book.'

Lacy Johnson, author of *The Other Side*

'*My Father's Glass Eye* signals the arrival of an exceptionally fine new voice.'

Alexandra Styron, author of *Reading My Father*

'An absolutely beautiful exploration of family, grief, memory, and madness, this book is outstanding.'

Jamie Thomas, Women & Children First

Jeannie Vanasco is the acclaimed author of *My Father's Glass Eye*. Her writing has appeared in the *Times Literary Supplement*, *The New York Times*, and the *New Yorker*. She lives in Baltimore where she works as an Assistant Professor of English at Towson University. *Things We Didn't Talk About When I Was a Girl* is her second, deeply moving memoir. Find out more: www.jeannievanasco.com

MY
FATHER'S
GLASS
EYE

a memoir

JEANNIE VANASCO

DUCKWORTH

This edition first published in the United Kingdom by
Duckworth in 2019
Duckworth, an imprint of Prelude Books ltd
1 Golden Court, Richmond
TW9 1EU United Kingdom
www.preludebooks.co.uk
For bulk and special sales please contact
info@preludebooks.co.uk

© 2017 Jeannie Vanasco

A catalogue record for this book is available from the British Library.

Text design and typesetting by Geethik

Printed and bound in Great Britain by Clays Ltd, Elcograf S.p.A.

9780715653777

The hero is a feeling, a man seen
As if the eye was an emotion,
As if in seeing we saw our feeling
In the object seen . . .

From "Examination of the Hero in a
Time of War" by Wallace Stevens

My parents raised me in a white-sided saltbox house, the sort children draw in crayon. Years before we lived there, it had been cut in half and moved across town. We never learned why.

PART ONE

ONE

The night before he died, I promised my dad I would write a book for him. I was harboring profound confidence charged with profound grief.

The day after he died, I was supposed to turn in a paper about *Hamlet*. My professor granted me an extension. I focused on the development of Hamlet's grief for his father, and the question of madness.

One week after he died, I was supposed to take a sociology exam. My professor did not grant me an extension. I did not read the chapter about grief, though I answered the questions about grief correctly.

One month after he died, I wrote on my arms and legs until they turned black: "before I lost him he lost his left eye I left his left eye he is not his glass eye the i left him."

Nine years after he died, in an attempt to organize my thoughts, I started keeping several color-coded binders labeled "Dad,"

"Mom," "Jeanne," and "Mental Illness." Within each binder are categories, such as "Vision" and "Voice." "Jeannie" isn't a binder. I'm "Mental Illness."

DAD

I remember almost nothing from before my dad lost vision in his left eye—as if my life begins there. Years of my life appear full of shadows, but the night I disappeared is full of light.

My parents and I were playing the Memory Game. The goal was to find among all the cards two that matched. I was four. It was my dad's turn.

I waited what felt like a long time for him to choose a card as he closed one eye, then the other. When the right eye closed I disappeared.

"I close my right eye," he told my mom, "and I can't see Jeannie."

I closed my left eye, then my right, a game of illusions that moved objects, moving my dad an inch each time.

•

In photos, my dad is almost always looking at me, never at the camera. This made it hard to choose his obituary photo. In the newspaper, my mom and I were cropped out of it.

In the original photo, the three of us are at the kitchen table. My dad is sixty-six, my mom is forty-six, and I'm four. In a month, at that same wooden table, his left eye will stop working, but in the photo his eyes are fine—a deep brown so piercing they seem to look right inside me and know me. What hair he has is white and blends in with the white curtains behind him. His olive skin shows wrinkles. His forehead and cheeks have a greasy shine. He looks strong, thick-waisted but not fat. He wears belted gray slacks and a crisp white button-down shirt. Underneath his shirt likely hangs his gold necklace of the Holy Family. He stands behind my mom, leaning in and smiling. She's smiling too and holding me on her lap. With her clear tan skin and thick curly blonde hair, she looks young enough, is young enough, to be his daughter.

And then there's me. At four years old, I want—or will remember wanting—one blue eye the shade of my mom's, and one brown eye the shade that my dad and I share. But in a month, his eye doctor will tell me, "You have your dad's eyes," and I'll never want a blue eye again. My wavy brown hair is pulled into a ponytail tied with a blue ribbon. My dad likely tied that ribbon. When I was a child, he did my hair—trimmed, brushed, and often braided it. He'd been a barber when he was young, and throughout my childhood he seemed young.

Worried that other children would tease me about his age, he tried to color his hair dark brown the year I started kindergarten; it turned deep red, and until it faded he wore a hat everywhere—including at home.

MOM

Almost every day my mom and I talk on the phone, and almost every day we talk about my dad. He finds his way into the conversation, or rather we lead him there: "I remember this one time your father . . ." "How did Dad tell the story . . ." "I wish I could have him back."

She still lives in Sandusky, Ohio, in the house he died in. I live in New York, not far from the house where he was born.

"You only wanted him," my mom says. "You wouldn't stop crying unless you had him. You wouldn't let me put you to bed, read you stories. You were with him all day. You were used to him. I'd call from work and ask what he was doing. 'I'm making Jeannie animals out of paper.' Or 'I'm teaching Jeannie how to twirl spaghetti.'"

She pauses. "He saw how unhappy I was. 'She needs her mother,' he told me. So I agreed to quit working. You were a year old. I was worried about money, but he said we could make do on his retirement and Social Security."

And we did. No one could say I did without. I had dogs and turtles and bunnies. I attended private school. I practiced ballet at a dance studio near the lake, learned how to paint fish and birds on Saturdays in an artist's home. Every month, I accompanied my dad to the bank where he bought savings bonds in my name.

"For your college someday," he said.

DAD

I remember only one visit to my dad's eye doctor—though my mom tells me there were more.

My dad sat in the middle of a white room, peering into a coal-black lens machine with his left eye. A circle of lights shone over him. I stayed at my mom's feet with a coloring book.

His doctor leaned cautiously into him, prodding the eye with a wand of light.

The doctor left the room and returned with a nurse. She motioned for me to follow her into the hallway. I did, and she closed the door behind us.

"Your grandfather is a brave man," she said.

She told me to stay where I was and disappeared into another room before I could say, "He's my dad."

I cracked open the door and looked at him. The doctor was pressing a needle into my dad's eye, and my dad didn't flinch.

MOM

"How did Dad accept the loss of his eye?" I ask my mom. "Did he accept it?"

"Yes, I think so. I don't know if you remember how he used to throw up constantly and couldn't walk up and down the steps. We had that sofa bed in the living room and he had to sleep down there all the time. It was like a pressure that built in his eye. He either had to live with it or have the eye taken out. So he said, 'Let's have the eye taken out.'"

I remember the hospital felt a long way from home.

I remember we stopped on the way and ate hamburgers in what used to be a bank. Chandeliers hung above us.

"Do you remember the priest in his room, the other patient?" she asks.

"No."

"The priest told your dad, 'I don't know if I could accept that,' and your dad said, 'Well, what difference does it make if I accept it? It's not going to change it.' He was very brave about it. Your dad was very brave."

DAD

Almost every week when I was a child, my parents either walked or drove me to the library, a turreted limestone building. One small room, on the grown-up side, featured a glass floor.

"You won't fall through," my parents took turns promising.

My dad would offer me his hand, and I'd tap my foot against the glass and say something like, "Next time."

But I wanted to walk bravely across the glass. And I want to say his loss of his left eye gave me courage. I knew his surgery meant he was brave, because that's what his nurses and doctors told me.

But I forget my immediate feelings about conquering the glass floor, about seeing—for the first time—the room's books about wars, physics, and clouds. I remember, though, waving at my dad from across the room, and returning to him.

MOM

"Degenerative eye disease, maybe?" my mom says on the phone. "Advanced glaucoma? The doctor said it happens to something like one in a million people."

"What happened exactly?"

"Your dad's tear ducts were closed and clotted with blood, and the doctors couldn't get them to drain. I don't know what you call it."

"Try to remember."

"I can't."

DAD

Not long after he lost his eye, I lost one of my front teeth. My parents told me to put it underneath my pillow.

For the tooth fairy, they said.

In the morning, instead of my tooth I found a one-hundred-dollar bill. I ran down the steps, two at a time.

"The tooth fairy gave me a hundred dollars!" I shouted.

My parents exchanged looks.

"Wow," my mom said. "I bet the tooth fairy thought she gave you ten dollars."

My dad opened his wallet.

"Her mistake," I said.

MOM

He built me toys and shelves.

"He wanted to prove himself," my mom says after I call again, asking about his eye. "One morning—this was a few weeks after his surgery—he started building you a dollhouse. I was washing dishes when he came inside with a piece of wood stuck in his stomach. 'I almost lost my hand,' he told me. You weren't there. You were in school."

"Was it serious?" I ask.

"The wood wasn't in deep. I helped him pull it out. But it hurt his confidence."

At our next garage sale, his saw shared a table with clothes I'd outgrown. I was assigning prices with our sticker gun.

"How much for the saw?" I asked him.

The question seemed so inconsequential then.

DAD

I watched a woman paint my dad's new eye. Spools of red thread, shiny blades, small jars of paint, and brushes thinner than my watercolor brushes were arranged on her long desk.

It was important the new eye look like, rather than be, an exact match, because no one's eyes match perfectly.

As she painted, she looked at my dad's real eye, then down at the glass eye, then back at his real eye.

"What do you think?" she asked me when it was finished.

I looked at my dad, then down at his new eye.

MOM

I call my mom again.

"Am I remembering right?" I ask her. "Did I watch someone paint Dad's new eye?"

"You watched," my mom says. "And I remember what you said when it was done: 'It looks real.'"

DAD

"I can't see out of my left eye," I told him after he received his glass eye. "Do you think I need a glass eye?"

"Are you lying?" he asked gently.

"I want to be like you," I said.

TWO

I've written hundreds of pages about my dad: poems, essays, short stories, a novel, several versions of a memoir—all titled *The Glass Eye*.

Here on my writing desk is an anatomical model of the human eye. Lifting off its upper hemisphere reveals painted veins that look like blue and pink branches. The white body inside the eye is mostly transparent, mostly scratched. According to the gold label on the pinewood stand, the eye was crafted by a Chicago company that also manufactured maps and globes. It makes sense; my dad's eye is my world.

But why does his eye matter?

Only after he died did it obsess me. Describing my dad through the metaphor of his eye comes easy; encapsulating him in plain language feels impossible.

My dad's eye was plastic, but sometimes I call it glass. Glass implies the ability to be broken.

What if I write a book about the history of artificial eyes?

What if I write a book that avoids even mentioning the eye?

What if I write the book I want to write, the one about my love for my dad?

What other book is there?

I need to pan out, not focus so much on his eye. I haven't even described the town where we lived. My dad loved Sandusky.

DAD

If you spread out a map of Sandusky, Ohio, you can see that at many intersections you can turn left or slightly left, continue straight, or turn slightly right or right. Twenty-five thousand people live there, but every summer more than three million visit for Cedar Point, the local amusement park. When passing car accidents in town, I often looked at the license plates; they almost always belonged to cars registered elsewhere. A former city manager once told me that some of the streets form the Masonic symbol. I noticed MASON printed on several limestone and sandstone buildings after that. My dad, when he was young, drove a taxi in New York, yet when he first moved into the house where my mom has lived much of her adult life, he often would get lost in town.

MOM

"This one morning," she tells me on the phone, "maybe the same week he moved in, he left the house to pick up milk and came home five hours later. He couldn't remember our address or our phone number."

The house had belonged to her and her first husband, who she married at eighteen.

"Did it bother Dad," I ask her, "that you'd lived here with someone else?"

"No, but originally we'd planned to move to Arizona, or someplace warm like that, after we married. But then you were born, and he immediately started putting away money for you. It made sense to stay. And he loved this house."

"What did he love about it?"

"He liked that it was in a quiet neighborhood. Rarely did a car go by. The double garage gave him plenty of room to build things. The yard had enough room for a nice garden, your playhouse, your swing set. If you remember, we'd play badminton in the backyard, the three of us, behind the garage. He loved sitting on the back porch, drinking a glass of scotch, and looking out at all the flowers and shrubs. He wanted to be buried in the backyard."

•

Whenever my friends called our house tiny, I tried to ignore them. They lived in sparsely furnished houses with pale furniture and tall ceilings and pet gates. No one wore shoes past the front door. Their living rooms were off-limits. Their family rooms looked like their living rooms—only friendlier. Their coffee tables absolutely required coasters. Our coasters sat underneath one side of our furniture. Sometimes we used blocks of wood.

"We have them because our house is crooked," my mom explained when I asked why no one else kept their coasters there.

We never could hang a picture straight. So as a kid, when I drew landscapes, I started with a crooked horizon.

DAD

"You know there's a 216 West Boalt?" visitors to our garage sales often told us.

We lived at 216 East Boalt Street. West Boalt and East Boalt never meet, and the sign for West Boalt says only Boalt Street.

"New York has the grid," I once overheard my dad explain, and I was briefly reminded that he'd lived there; he rarely mentioned it.

"Do you miss it?" I once asked him.

"Not at all," he answered. "Sandusky is heaven."

•

"Across from the baseball field and IAB," we often included in our garage sale listings in the *Sandusky Register*. After the newspaper raised its ad rates, charging by the letter, we shortened our directions to "near IAB." Most people in town knew that IAB stood for Italian American Beneficial Club.

MOM

"Little Italy my ass," I heard my mom mumble the night she tore the green Welcome to Little Italy sign out of the ground. I was seven and couldn't understand why the sign made her so angry. I liked it. The city had placed it right by our driveway, next to the stop sign on the corner where we lived. I ran inside and told my dad what she was doing.

"Go tell her the cops are going to come for her," he said. "That's city property."

I begged my mom to leave the sign alone.

"The police!" I yelled.

"Go back inside or they'll take you too," she said.

The next evening, at our kitchen table, I asked my parents why they were so quiet.

"I'm angry at your father," she said.

"When people are angry," he explained to me, "they say things they'll come to regret."

Shortly after they married, they made a pact that if either of them was angry at the other, they'd say nothing until their anger had cooled. Usually, if my mom was angry, she'd reorganize kitchen drawers and cabinets, and my dad and I knew better than to ask where the forks had gone. If she felt stressed, she'd rearrange our furniture. This time, though, she hadn't moved the couch or the silverware. This time she'd yanked a heavy metal sign—pole and all—out of the ground.

"What are you angry about?" I asked.

My dad and I looked at her for an answer.

"Do you know?" she asked him.

"I don't know," he said.

"Well, I don't remember," she said.

They laughed, and I laughed, and our uneven house became idyllic again.

DAD

Late summer nights when I was a child, my parents sat on the rusted aluminum glider on our back porch and told stories about their lives. My mom as a girl once put her little "tattletale" sister on a slow-moving train.

"She was sucking her thumb and waving from a train car when a neighbor saw and went running to my mother," she said, "and did I ever get beat."

My dad learned how to cut hair when he was a boy by practicing on homeless men—"bums," he called them, with a fondness in his voice.

"Okay. Time for bed," they'd say and I'd pretend to go upstairs.

Then I'd sneak back down, hide with my mutt, Gigi, in the pantry, press my ear against the screen door, and listen. That was when they told the good stories: my mom chased her abusive first husband from the house with a butcher knife; my dad was arrested for gambling with his mafia friends when he was seventeen, and his father refused to bail him out of jail. Later, when my dad was out of earshot, I'd ask my mom about his stories.

"Dad told it to me," I'd lie. "Can you remind me how it goes?"

She said that when he was in junior high, he started sweeping hair at his father's barbershop. His father told him, "Never open the door to the back room." So one day my dad pretended he was sweeping hair by the door, and cracked it open—just enough to see in. A man was roped to a chair with his mouth gagged. His hand was in a vise that another man slowly turned. A third man sat in the corner, eating a sandwich. My dad closed the door and returned to sweeping hair.

"What's a vise?" I asked my mom.

"You know, sort of like the thing your dad has on his workbench, that he uses to hold down wood while he cuts it," my mom explained. "Only this was something a little different. They ground up the guy's hand in it."

Another story I overheard and that my mom later confirmed: after my dad caught his first wife in bed with her cousin's husband, his friends offered to throw her off a roof. "We'll frame it as a suicide," they told him. My dad refused: "I can't. That's the mother of my children." I remember thinking: *My dad is an upstanding man.* I didn't think: *Of course you shouldn't throw your adulterous spouse off a roof.*

MOM

Just as I did when I was a child, I ask my mom for more stories about my dad.

"He painted warships in Brooklyn during World War II," she reminds me, "and developed throat cancer from the asbestos the navy used."

Before I was born, doctors removed his left vocal cord to prevent the cancer from spreading. I wish I had a recording of his voice. I remember standing in a hard hat and tool belt, watching my dad sand a piece of wood. He said something to me, and his voice disappeared into the sound of sandpaper.

"He knew how scratchy his voice sounded," my mom says. "He was careful not to raise his voice, especially around you—he was afraid of scaring you. Then he was afraid of the eye falling out and scaring you. Poor guy."

This reminds her of a story.

"One evening we were eating spaghetti at the kitchen table and his eye fell out and rolled across the table. 'Dad, your eye popped out,' you told him and kept on eating," my mom says. "You were just a kid. It didn't faze you."

"I don't really remember that," I say.

"I do. He felt so awful about it. I told him, 'She loves you. She doesn't care.'"

DAD

At Cedar Point, my dad went on the rides with me—even the one where we raced in separate potato sacks down a giant sloping slide. Sometimes people pointed and laughed. "Look at that old man," they'd say. For the fast rides and the tall ones, my mom usually waited at the bottom. After the Blue Streak, the park's oldest roller coaster, he was covering his left eye with his hand.

"Is it still there?" he asked my mom.

"It's there," she said, and they both laughed.

•

But more than the amusement park, the Erie County Landfill was my favorite place when I was a kid.

"The dump, the dump, the dump," I'd say as I buckled myself into the car.

Because my parents' friends knew how much I loved the landfill, and even though each resident was allotted only so many free trips there, they gave us some of their free tickets. I loved seeing what people threw away. I remember wondering if the trash looked as beautiful to my dad as it did to me.

"Well she's not too hard to please," he told my mom.

•

And I loved seeing my dad unwrap the presents I gave him. One Christmas, I made him a wooden plaque out of scrap wood I found in the garage. I wrote in marker: "Best Dad," or something like that. I put it inside an old power-tool box and wrapped it. After unwrapping it and seeing the power-tool box, he said, "You shouldn't have."

I worried he'd be disappointed when he found the wooden plaque instead of a power tool. I shyly told him to look inside the box. He did, and he started to cry.

"Now this is amazing," he said.

When he died, the plaque was still hanging above his workstation in the garage. I can't look at what I made him. At some point, it may end up in the garbage, at the landfill—where he and I shook our heads at what people threw away.

•

Our garage was my dad's magician's hat. My mom helped him carry out new, amazing objects: bookshelves taller than them, rose arches, birdhouses with as many as eight different entrances, dollhouses shaped like our house. Too enormous to fit through our back door, my favorite dollhouse required him to remove the door from its hinges. In summer months, the dollhouse stayed outside. One day he mounted it on wheels.

A "mobile home," he called it.

The roof, made of real asphalt like ours, lifted off to reveal an attic. He added screens and shutters to all the windows. He wallpapered each room. He used free samples of linoleum and carpet from a local flooring store; the saleswoman assumed we were redecorating our house. He even made a staircase and cut a hole in the second floor.

"I don't want to make your dolls have to fly from floor to floor," he said.

Before our garage sales, I parked the dollhouse out of view, usually on our back porch. At one sale, however, a woman noticed the dollhouse from our driveway. I was walking around with my sticker gun, lowering prices, when I saw her playing with the blue shutters. I ran over.

"This for sale?" she asked.

"No," I told her. "My dad made it."

She removed a pen and checkbook from her purse and offered me $1,000.

"It's not for sale," I said.

"Where's your dad?"

I pointed at him.

"That old man in the eye patch?"

"He made it," I said, "and with only one eye."

She stooped and patted me on the shoulder.

"You're very lucky," she said and walked away.

My dad came over and asked what she had wanted. I told him.

"Go get her! I'll make you a new one."

But she'd already left.

•

He built a one-room house for me in the backyard; he fenced in a private yard behind it and taught me how to manage my own garden. I had my own mailbox where my dad regularly delivered letters that he and my mom had written. He made a cement walkway leading to our back porch and before the cement dried we wrote "Dad and Jeannie," drew a heart. We left our handprints.

•

He made our red picket fence out of scrap wood from a lumberyard where on its opening day I rode a pony and won a goldfish.

•

Passersby slowed down their cars and pointed at our yard. Finches always seemed to be splashing in our birdbaths, and strange colorful flowers appeared unexpectedly.

"Did you plant that?" my parents asked one another.

The answer was often no.

•

One afternoon, I was in the driveway, practicing how to ride a bike.

"Don't go too close to the street," my dad told me.

I was bad at braking, and he'd run and catch up with me. Mostly, though, my dad kept pace, but when he spotted a sports car speeding toward our corner with no clear intention of obeying the stop sign, he shouted and ran toward the car. The driver slammed his brakes. I was in the middle of the driveway. I jumped off my bike, chased after my dad, and watched as he reached one hand through the driver's open window and said, "You'd be worth going to prison for." He pointed at me, and then at the stop sign. That evening, he began building a long lattice fence to stretch across our driveway. A few days later, he mounted the fence on wheels. He demonstrated how it worked. My mom and I clapped.

Now, when I think of the fence, I think of Jeanne.

THREE

In the Memory Game you're expected to find two matching cards. My dad's left eye and his right didn't perfectly match. The *i* and the eye don't perfectly match, but they sound the same. Jeanne and Jeannie sound the same, but we don't perfectly match. I could write this story chronologically and divide it into three parts titled "eye," "*i*," and "I."

But I worry that I lose authority as a storyteller if I recall memories from age four. I could preface some of those memories with "I remember." Or, in memoir, is such subjectivity implied? Like "I see" and "I hear," "I remember" is almost always an unnecessary filter. Maybe I can preface the more detailed memories with "I remember"—a defense against any reader who thinks, *There's no way she remembers playing the Memory Game when she was four,* or *It couldn't have been the Memory Game—it's so symbolic. It feels forced.*

Do I need to be more selective with direct dialogue, or introduce hindsight perspective, or lean on my mom's memories? I'll keep some of her in the present tense. I'll show how I often ask her questions, such as: "Did it happen this way?" "What was his illness called?" "Did Dad accept the loss of his eye?" But if I excerpt conversations with her that concern only him, then it looks like I care less about her life stories.

I'll write another book after this, a book for her.

JEANNE

Not once did my dad say Jeanne's name in my eighteen years with him. My mom did when I was eight.

I was dancing in my bedroom with an unlit candle when she called me downstairs. My teacher, Sister Paulina, had asked three second-grade girls to lead our First Communion ceremony with a dance. The dance required me to hold a candle above my head, and I was terrified of setting the church on fire. I practiced at home almost every day for a month.

When I walked into the living room, my dad was in his chair, holding a small white box. As my mom explained that he had a dead daughter named Jeanne (pronounced the same as my name) "without an *i*," he opened the box and looked away. Inside was a medal Jeanne had received from a church "for being a good person," my mom said. My dad said nothing. I said nothing. I stared at the medal.

Later that day, in the basement, my mom told me Jeanne had died in a car accident when she was sixteen. I sat on the steps as my mom folded clothes and confided what she knew.

Two other girls were in the car. The car could seat three people in front. Jeanne sat between the driver and the other passenger. The driver tried to pass a car, then hesitated and tried to pull back into her lane. She lost control and the car crashed. Jeanne was the only one who died.

"Your father blames himself," my mom said. "He can't talk about it."

"Why?" I asked.

"He gave her permission to go out that night."

Jeanne had asked him if she could see a movie with her friends. He asked what her mother had said. "She said to ask you." He said it was fine, she could see the movie. He had no idea his first wife had already said no. He and his first wife weren't speaking.

"Did you know his first wife?" I asked.

"No, he was divorced long before I met him. All this happened in New York."

It happened near Newburgh, where he and his first family had lived. I knew only Ohio. In my mind all of New York was made of skyscrapers, taxicabs, and car accidents.

"What did Jeanne look like?"

My mom said she'd never seen a photo.

•

I painted portraits of Jeanne in watercolor. I titled them *Jeanne*. My art teacher told me she was disappointed that "such a good student could misspell her name." From then on, I included an *i*.

•

"I wanted to tell you about Jeanne before that," my mom says, after I ask why she told me when she did. "But your dad, he worried that you'd misinterpret his intentions. I told him, 'She's going to find out someday. Don't you think it's better she hear it from us?'"

"Did Dad have any photos of Jeanne?"

"No. He told me his ex-wife wouldn't let him have any. But for some reason, she gave him the medal."

•

Throughout my baby scrapbook, I'm referred to as "Barbara Jean," "Jean," "Jeanie," and "Jeannie." In one letter, my dad calls me "My Darling Daughter Barbara Jean." In a letter to my mom, he calls me "Jeanie" and "Jeannie." My parents had planned to name me Jeanne.

"That or Jean Marie, actually," my mom says. "Her given name was Jean Marie. She went by Jeanne. Your father simply saw the name as a sign of respect. He even spoke with a priest about our naming you after her, and the priest encouraged him to do so, provided he never compare you. 'I would never do that,' your father said."

But while my mom was asleep after having just given birth, he named me Barbara Jean, after my mom. When he told her what he'd done, she said, "That's no name for a baby." She thought Barbara was too old-fashioned. That, and two Barbaras in one house would be confusing.

"When I told him I wasn't calling you Barbara, he got this sad look on his face. He meant to do something sweet," she says. "He always had good intentions."

Legally my name remained Barbara Jean, but my parents called me Jeannie. My dad added the *i*.

"Just said he was adding an *i*," my mom says. "He never explained it."

•

I remember the spring day that I stood alone in the corner of the school playground, thinking about Jeanne. Cars passed by with their windows open. I often wondered if my dad thought about Jeanne every time he drove our car. A classmate, another second-grade girl, asked what I was doing.

"My half sister died," I told her.

"I have a stepsister."

I tried to explain the difference between a half-sibling and a stepsibling.

"We share the same dad," I said.

"I didn't know you had a half sister."

"Four of them," I said, or maybe I said "three." I didn't know if Jeanne counted, or if she counted more because she was dead.

•

I have no clear memory of learning about Jeanne's sisters—Carol, Arlene, and Debbie—but I know my parents told me about them before I learned about Jeanne. Arlene is the only one I knew throughout my childhood. She lived in New York. She visited us four times in Ohio—five, if you count when our dad was dying.

"Arlene is beautiful," I told my mom after Arlene's first visit.

Arlene's dark brown eyes matched her hair. Thick and wavy, it fell just past her shoulders. Later I'd show photographs of Arlene

to boys I liked; I wanted them to think that I'd be beautiful someday, like her.

"She was a model once," my mom said. "I think she modeled
wedding dresses for a catalogue."

Arlene often called, wrote letters. She mailed me unusual
presents: hangers with illustrated wooden cat heads, vials of
sand from Jerusalem, a pair of earrings that looked like pale
orange pearls. She even trained her cockatiel to say "Happy
birthday, Jeannie." She sent a video of it. I wrote thank-you
letters; they went through several drafts. I wanted my cursive
to look perfect.

Carol and Debbie I'd never seen, not even in photographs.
Debbie was a hairdresser in New York, and Carol owned a candy
shop in Rhode Island. Carol, the oldest, was my mom's age. Beyond that, I knew nothing.

Once, while my dad was on the downstairs rotary, I listened
through the upstairs rotary. I was in the second grade and often
eavesdropped. I could hear one of his daughters—not Arlene,
I'd have recognized her voice—yelling. My dad mentioned me,
and she yelled more. I quietly set the phone on my bedroom
carpet. I could still hear her. When no more sound came from
the receiver, I looked through the grate in my bedroom floor.
My dad was at the dining room table, his head in his hands.

"They were mad your father had his first marriage annulled,"
my mom explains. "It was after your First Communion. You
asked him why he couldn't take Communion with you. He said
it was because he was divorced. It's a man-made rule—that you
can't take Communion if you've been divorced. If you annul the
marriage, the church basically says the marriage never existed.

His daughters took it personally. He didn't mean anything against them. He wasn't disowning them. He did it for you."

•

Jeanne would come between me and almost everything I did. I studied harder. I researched the lives of the saints and how I might model their behavior. I sat before my bedroom mirror with a notebook and documented my appearance and what exactly I needed to fix. I needed to be a smart, kind, beautiful daughter.

I tried not to hear her name when he said my own.

•

I followed my parents to their graves. Rain made it difficult to find our way.

"Where do I walk?" I asked, afraid of disrespecting the dead.

My mom told me to follow her. We passed a smaller fenced-in area where fresh flowers and toys were at almost every grave.

"The children's cemetery," she explained.

My dad stood farther ahead of us, underneath a tree. He motioned us toward him.

I looked down at two headstones printed with my parents' names and birth years: "Terry J Vanasco, 1922," and "Barbara J Vanasco, 1942."

"Where do I go?" I asked.

"You might have a husband someday," my mom said. "You'll want to be buried next to him."

"But I want to be with you and Dad."

•

I call my mom, ask if she remembers that day in the cemetery.

"We took you to see the graves?"

"That's what I remember," I say.

DAD

After Jeanne died, my dad bought burial plots for himself and his wife next to the plot for Jeanne. When he and his first wife divorced, she demanded that he forfeit his plot because she didn't want him buried next to their daughter. He agreed. Soon after the divorce, he went to court again, this time for beating up "a bum" on the street.

"Why should you be alive?" my dad asked him. "You're not working and my daughter's dead."

The judge remembered my dad and let him go.

My dad's sister Anna told all this to my mom, who at some point shared it with me. I don't know if I learned this story before or after seeing my parents' headstones, but the two stories juxtaposed together make sense, writing-wise. Still, I call my mom, ask if she remembers when she told me about my dad losing his burial plot.

"I don't," she says, "but did I ever tell you: when I went with your dad to his father's funeral—this was a couple years before you were born—the funeral director told me about your dad losing his cemetery plot. The director said, 'In all the years I've worked here, I've never heard of anything like it—denying a man burial next to his daughter.' Your dad's ex-wife eventually did offer him the plot—this was when you were a little girl—but your dad refused it. He said, 'I have a family here.'"

MOM

It was my parents' twelfth wedding anniversary. I was ten. A snowstorm swept through Sandusky. We had plans to celebrate at home that night. We were in our car leaving the grocery parking lot when my mom abruptly told him to stop the car.

She left it, slammed her door, and opened mine.

"We're walking home," she told me.

My dad looked back at me.

"Come on," she said. "I'm teaching you a lesson."

"What did I do?" I asked.

"I'm teaching you you don't need a man."

I told her there was a snowstorm. It was too cold to walk home. Our house felt far away.

"Stay with him if you want," she said and began to leave us.

I apologized to my dad and ran after her.

My dad slowly followed in the car with the front passenger window down.

"It's a blizzard," he said.

She ignored him.

I asked her why she was angry, and she ignored me.

He pleaded for us to get in the car. Home was at least two miles away.

She yelled at him to leave us alone. He looked at me, and I looked down at my boots. When I looked up, our car was disappearing into the falling snow.

"What if he dies in a car accident?" I asked.

"He'll be fine."

"But there's ice."

"He won't die."

I watched my breath chill before me and disappear.

We walked in silence along the shoulder of Milan Road. When I looked behind us, snow had already covered our tracks. Snow plows rumbled by. A few cars came and went. A man offered us a ride and my mom waved him off.

"We're almost home," she lied.

The man drove away.

"Your father doesn't trust me," she said.

The friendly man who worked in checkout at the grocery store, my dad thought was too friendly, she explained.

My dad often told us to wait in the car while he checked out. I always thought he was being a gentleman, bringing the groceries to us.

"Your father doesn't trust anyone," she said.

"What about me?"

"You're different."

•

When we reached our house, he was at the kitchen table, his head in his hands.

"Dad," I said.

I yanked off my boots and ran to him.

My mom walked past us and into the basement. He followed her, and I went into the bathroom and lifted the door to the laundry chute. I heard my dad apologize.

That evening at dinner, they smiled at one another and held hands.

•

"Sometimes he drove me nuts with his possessiveness," my mom says when I ask about the snowstorm. "His father was the same way, apparently. Your dad's mother would go to the grocery store, and your dad's father would time her. Your dad thought it was horrible, but then he went and did the same sort of thing to me." She pauses. "After you left for college, your dad and I were on the back porch—and he asked if I regretted our marriage. 'Of course not,' I told him. 'Why would you ask me that?' He said he knew how unreasonable he'd been. He said he was sorry. He said he was afraid of losing me. Your dad would have been happy, just the three of us, in a cabin out in the woods. He said you and I were all he needed."

FOUR

I open a cardboard box packed with my journals and medical records. The journals contain a mess of fragments and diagrams and outlines. On one page is a circle of arrows, and inside the circle is a handwritten sentence in tiny script: "I can't write." Strips of paper are glued or stapled to some pages. On each strip is a typed sentence from past writing projects.

One strip reads: "A strip of Italian widows." A blue arrow points to some notes in the right margin: "strip of paper/strip of street" and "East Boalt/I bolted East." After my dad died, only Italian widows lived on East Boalt Street. On that same page, I drew my childhood home and wrote "Metaphor" on all the windows. I cut an opening where the front door would be. Behind the door, stapled on the next page, is a letter, which I photocopied, from my dad to my mom:

> *Sweetheart,*
>   *Would you believe I asked our daughter if she would make me an Easter card for you, because I didn't feel well enough*

to go out to buy you one. Her reply was "Don't worry Dad.
I'll make one for you." So that was why we were very secretive
when you walked in the room and I was spelling her the word
WIFE. She sure is something for just a little 6 yr. old. She's
more like 16 yrs. PS: I think we should have Jeannie make
all our holiday and birthday cards and the money can be put
away for her education.

Your Ever Loving Husband

The only part visible through the door: "Don't worry Dad."

Some of my sentences are crossed out, but I don't know why: "~~We lived a few blocks away from the railroad tracks. At night, train whistles lulled me to sleep.~~" On the next page, I sketched our staircase and wrote memories climbing across and up its steps. Underneath the staircase I wrote "I can't sleep I can't sleep I can't sleep."

How can I capture mania on the page and still make sense?

And forget the medical records. I lied to my doctors so many times I can't trust those.

MENTAL ILLNESS

I remember standing on the top of our stairway when I was eleven, or maybe twelve, and hearing an unfamiliar voice. It said *Jeannie*, or maybe *Jeanne*. My mind filled with loud, hurried thoughts, and just as suddenly emptied, like a flock of birds scattering from a field. I looked at my portraits framed on the wall, the chronology of my childhood. The farther down I looked, the younger I became.

I called out for my mom. She appeared at the bottom of the steps, holding a rag.

"What's wrong?" she asked.

I asked if she had called my name, and she said no. She was cleaning the kitchen floor.

"Where's Dad?"

He was in the garage, building a birdhouse, she said.

"What's wrong?" she repeated.

Had the voice called for me, or for my dead half sister?

"Nothing," I answered.

MOM

I call my mom just to chat, and she mentions she's reading a book about feng shui.

"Our house breaks almost every rule," she says. "Your main door isn't supposed to open in front of your staircase. This book says it creates huge amounts of negative energy. If the door and staircase are too close, like ours are, then you need a feng shui consultant."

My mom decorated the staircase every Christmas. She'd wrap gold garland around the handrail and each baluster. She'd put stuffed reindeer and Santas between some of the balusters. I'd run down the steps on Christmas morning, and Gigi would follow. We'd give Gigi wrapped bones and watch her chew and paw through the paper while we took turns opening our presents around the big artificial tree. When I was in junior high, I opened the power-tool box, the same one I'd wrapped my dad's plaque in, and inside were twenty books I'd wanted, mostly novels that I'd seen older students reading for class: *Catch-22*, *Great Expectations*, *To Kill a Mockingbird.*

DAD

That same Christmas, I gave my dad an iced tea maker, and he returned it and gave me back the money.

"Save this," he said. "You don't need to buy me anything. Just make or write me something."

JEANNE

"You can be anything you want to be," my dad said to me often.

Every month he led me into a small white room in the back of our bank where he'd show me colorful bonds in a safe-deposit box. Jeanne's medal was also in that box, in a white box of its own.

"This money is for your college someday," he'd remind me.
And inside the white box was what I tried to be.

•

Not once did my parents pressure me to be perfect, as I believed
Jeanne had been. Still, I tried to be. I had to be.

While my friends played kickball during recess, I sat on the
convent steps with the most unpopular girl—a kind, gangly bru-
nette who walked through the halls with her head down and always sat next to the teacher during Thursday morning mass.

"She's fun," I told my friends.

Actually, she spent most of our time together thanking me for
not ignoring her, like the other girls. She once asked how it was I
could smile as much as I did.

"I don't know," I lied, thinking of Jeanne.

"Your father said she was always smiling," my mom had told me.

I worried my kindness was disingenuous. I confessed it to a
priest. The priest told me not to be so hard on myself.

"Skip the rosary this time," he said.

I didn't understand.

"Skip it," he said.

MENTAL ILLNESS

In pursuit of perfection, I made a list. Kindness mattered first.
Secondly, intellect.

If I scored less than 100 percent on a test, I'd hide in a bathroom
stall, crying. In junior high, I started scratching my wrists. At night,

on my bed, I cut the soles of my feet with scissors. I told no one. I asked my teachers how I could improve as a student.

They arranged a conference with my parents.

But my scratches and cuts remained a secret.

"They told us we needed to stop being so hard on you," my mom says. "We told them, 'We're not doing it. She's doing it to herself.' We didn't understand it."

My behavior confused even me. There were vast fields of time that I forgot about Jeanne, or maybe I simply became lost in those fields.

•

Finally, beauty.

"You could wear a potato sack for a dress," my dad told me, "and still look beautiful."

Sometimes I glanced at my reflection in a store window or car mirror, but by fifth grade I avoided seeing myself as much as I could.

Yet the photographs of me that my dad kept in his wallet showed a pretty child: olive complexion, thick wavy dark hair, big dark eyes, thin.

"You're the most beautiful girl in the world," he often said. "Inside and out."

During Thursday morning mass, I compared the size of my thighs with those of the girl next to me. I wanted to be an altar girl yet worried how I'd look in the white robe.

My friends seemed as obsessed with their appearance as I was with mine. Before every gym class, the girls took turns weighing themselves in the locker room.

"How much do you weigh?" one girl asked me.

"I don't know," I lied.

The school nurse weighed me every week in her office. My teachers were concerned. My parents were concerned.

"I have a good metabolism," I told my parents, as I pushed my food around my plate.

When I did eat, it was only in front of them.

The girls in my grade played two games relentlessly: Miss America and Is She Pretty? In the first game, they reenacted on our playground Miss America competitions. The second game they played at sleepovers. One girl would leave the room while the others evaluated her appearance, beginning with her hair and working their way down to her legs. Then they voted.

DAD

Once, in fifth grade, I tried to leave the house in a skirt that hit a few inches above my knees.

"You can't wear that," my mom said.

I brushed past her into the kitchen where my dad was drinking coffee.

My dad looked at my skirt, then at me, then back at my skirt.

"I'll change," I said. "I'm sorry. I'll change."

JEANNE

One night my best friend and I sat on my bedroom floor with a Ouija board between us. The nuns at school called the planchette "the devil's tool," but almost every girl in my sixth-grade class owned a Ouija board. ("For Chrissake," my mom said after I told her what the nuns called it, "you can buy it at Toys 'R' Us. Come on, let's go get one.")

I confided to my friend that I wanted to talk to Jeanne.

"My half sister," I explained. "She was sixteen when she died."

"What do you want to ask her?"

"What did she want to be when she grew up?"

We touched our fingers to the planchette.

"Jeanne Vanasco," I said. "Jeanne Vanasco. Jeanne Vanasco."

I asked my friend to say Jeanne's name with me, and the planchette began to move: "I-A-M-J-E-A-N-N-I-E."

I let go.

"Why would you do that?" I said.

"What's wrong?"

"She doesn't have an *i* in her name."

"Oh," my friend said, and laughed.

DAD

"Do you want to go for a drive?" my dad asked me.

"Where?" I said.

"How about you and me feed the birds downtown?"

"Sure," I said.

We brought our dog, Gigi. Had my mom been home, she would have come, helped us shred up stale bread for the seagulls (if only we'd known it choked them), but she was shelving books at the library.

Naively I believed she now worked because she wanted to work. In reality, she'd taken the job because in fifth grade I joined the girls' basketball team. My parents could budget for my glasses, my braces, my regular checkups, but not a broken limb. I'd have done something low-risk, like chess club, had I known why she accepted the job.

My dad drove, and cars honked and passed us. Their drivers rolled down their windows and cursed.

"Dad, I think you need to drive faster."

"I drove plenty fast in New York. They can go around me if they're in such a hurry."

We drove by the courthouse, the carousel museum, and the sculpture of a boy in overalls, holding his leaking right boot in the center of a big fountain. The fountain fascinated my dad, the same way cows and country roads fascinated him.

Our car circled the library a few times, slowing when we passed the entrance.

I remembered my mom's words in the snowstorm: "Your father doesn't trust me."

"The library building is nice, isn't it?" he said.

As we circled the library for what felt like the tenth time, I asked if he wanted to go inside.

"No," he told me. "Let's go feed the birds."

•

My dad took a computer class at the library, partly, probably, to be near my mom, and partly because he wanted to learn.

My parents had just bought me a computer. Neither knew how to use it. My mom preferred not to touch it.

"I'll mess it up," she said.

But my dad enrolled in a free class. While he practiced on a computer upstairs, in the media room where my mom sometimes shelved movie tapes, I read downstairs, near the glass floor.

After his first class ended, my dad told me that when the teacher said, "Move your mouse to the top of your screen," my dad lifted his mouse in the air and moved it around.

"No, no, Terry," the teacher told him. "You keep it on the mouse pad."

MOM

"After I started working," my mom tells me, "he was lonely. Me at work, you at school. He got so he only wanted to spend time with you and me. He didn't want to go anywhere without us. Well, you know how possessive he was. He was so jealous when I started working. He'd drive around the library, making sure I was there. You remember."

"I do."

"I get it—his first wife ran around on him, and it hurt his confidence. But I'd keep telling him, 'Terry, I love you. You're it for me. You're the one.' I wanted to be with him, but he and I agreed that I should work for the insurance. I know it was hard for him. He came from the generation where the man provided. But you started playing basketball. What if you broke your arm? We didn't want to tell you that you couldn't do something because of insurance. We'd been paying for your dentist and doctors out of pocket before that. If you remember, we took you to the dentist every six months. Your father and me never had that when we were kids. We wanted the best for you. Everything was for you, and that's how we wanted it. You didn't have the best of things. We didn't take vacations. But we were happy. I'd never been so happy in my life."

"Did I ever get mad at him?" I ask her. "Lose my temper?"

"With your dad?" she says. "No. With me, yes. I was the one who had to tell you no. He couldn't tell you no. If you wanted to sleep over at your friend's house and he didn't approve of that friend's parents, he'd tell me, 'You have to tell her she can't. Have her friend stay the night here.' Why do you think all those sleepovers with your friends were at our house? That's because he didn't trust people. He and I would get into such fights about that. He was so afraid of something happening to you. I told him, 'She's got to live in the world at some point. We're not always going to be around to protect her.' One time he became absolutely irrational about something related to you going out. You were a kid. He told me that if I didn't tell you no, he was leaving. I said, 'You know where the suitcases are.' You didn't see these arguments. You didn't know how strict he was."

"He lost Jeanne and his wife blamed him for it," I say. "It makes sense that he was so overprotective."

"I know," she says. "I just hated being the bad guy."

FIVE

To describe my dad accurately may mean displaying his flaws. To describe my dad fairly, the motivations beneath his flaws should be shown.

Because he lost a daughter, he became an overprotective father.

Because his first wife cheated on him, he became a jealous husband.

His motivations cancel his flaws, I reason.

Am I displaying my flaws enough?

After I learned about my dead namesake, I became a perfectionist—competitive with Jeanne, without fully, consciously, recognizing my motivation. I wanted to be good because I wanted to be as good as Jeanne.

I worry I'm shaping my childhood inaccurately, fabricating my feelings because of some need for conflict and character motivation. That by selecting a majority of Jeanne-related scenes I'm somehow ignoring the bulk of my childhood. That, and I worry I'm too easily swayed by the sonic impact of a line. "I tried not to hear her name when he said my own"—that sounds nice but it seems wrong. Or maybe I'm digging up feelings I tried to ignore. I worry by pulling Jeanne into the prose, I'm ruining my promise to my dad. The thought that Jeanne bothered me would destroy him.

I promised him a book, but not this book.

MOM

"You were a perfectionist for as long as I can remember," my mom says after I call and share my theory—that Jeanne possibly is why I worked so hard. "In preschool, you got so mad that you couldn't tie your shoes. You sat in the living room for hours—I'm not kidding—practicing. Your dad and I told you not to worry, to try again tomorrow, but you wouldn't listen. You were stubborn, like him. A perfectionist, like him. You sat there trying until you got it right. You didn't get that from me, that's for sure. This one time you even told us to ground you—for what I don't even remember. You were in kindergarten or first grade. Your dad and I were so confused."

DAD

My aunt Anna died in a car accident when I was in junior high. First his daughter, now his sister, I remember thinking.

"She didn't know what she was doing," my mom explained. "She grabbed the wheel from your uncle."

Anna had suffered from Alzheimer's. My uncle Tony survived, but he lost his arm, or maybe both arms.

Until I was in the third grade, she and Tony visited every year. She played dolls with me. Tony tap-danced with me. They stopped visiting, I later learned, because he was trying to hide Anna's Alzheimer's. We kept in touch by phone and mail. They sent gifts on holidays and birthdays: a small doll from Sicily, colorful barrettes, old coins.

The funeral would be in New York.

Arlene worked for the airlines. She arranged for my dad's plane ticket. My mom said that she and I would stay in Ohio while he attended the funeral. I didn't ask why. I assumed it was because his other daughters didn't want me there.

On the drive to the airport, I asked my dad if he could bring a parachute with him. I'd never flown before.

"People fly in planes every day," my mom assured me.

As we walked through the airport, I kept looking up at my dad. He promised to call when he reached New York.

As he disappeared into a long hallway, I ran to a big window and stared at the plane that would carry him away.

MOM

My dad didn't like returning to New York. Would it be more accurate to end that sentence with "not after living in Ohio" or "not after losing Jeanne"?

"This one time," my mom tells me, "we were driving to New York to visit. You weren't born yet. Six hours into the drive, your father started to panic. His hands were shaking. 'I don't want to go,' he said. I told him, 'We don't have to.' So we turned around and drove back to Ohio."

56

Another time, he could have returned to New York to collect settlement money for his throat cancer. Almost everyone who painted warships with him developed lung or throat cancer.

"He would've had to show up in New York to collect the money," my mom says. "His brother, Frank, had called him, tried to get him to come for the money—thousands of dollars. Your dad would have had to bring proof or talk with someone about the cancer. I can't remember. But he didn't want to go, and I told him he didn't have to. He pointed out that he'd smoked for fifty years. He quit smoking when you were born, just like that. He said, 'Who's to say I didn't get the throat cancer from smoking?' I told him, 'If you don't want to go, you don't have to. If it upsets you, the money isn't worth it.'"

DAD

When I was in junior high, he sold a car we had. It stalled at random times. Two teenage boys wanted it. They worked on cars. "I only want you to pay me for the price of the tires," my dad told them. "Those are brand-new tires. But you have to promise me you won't drive it. Use it for any parts that are still good."

He must have been thinking of Jeanne.

MENTAL ILLNESS

In junior high, I volunteered as a candy striper at the local hospital. I changed patients' sheets. I brought clean towels and mail. For patients with no visitors and no mail, I brought flowers and unsigned notes that read: "Feel better," "Thinking of you," and so on. Most patients were my dad's age, but he was still healthy. He could still garden and build things, like rose arches and birdhouses.

"You loved volunteering at that hospital," my mom says. "Your dad would drive you there, come back, and tell me how proud he was of you."

Some evenings I volunteered at the hospital's main desk, answering phone calls and sorting mail. Any mail to the psychiatric ward was to be put aside. Its patients could be dangerous, my boss explained. The other candy stripers called them "lunatics" and "crazies" who claimed to hear voices and see visions. I thought about the saints I studied in school. I thought about the voice and hurried thoughts on my stairway. What separated a saint from someone mad?

•

I'm not sure why, but I decided to hand-deliver mail to the psychiatric ward. I waited until its doors opened for a doctor ahead of me, and then I slipped in after. The ward looked enormous. A piano, couches, and card tables were on one side. The nurses' station was in the middle. And on the other side was a hallway of closed doors. The patients mostly resembled people in my town. Several played cards. Others surrounded a small television set. But there was one patient, seated by herself, her eyes fixed on the middle distance.

A nurse ran to me.

"You're not supposed to be here."

I apologized and handed her the envelopes.

I tried to open the doors, but she said she needed to do that.

I looked back at the empty gaze before I left. I could tell there was something wrong.

JEANNE

"Jeannie, they called your name."

I was sitting in the bleachers of a school gym several towns away. Hundreds of other junior high students from throughout Ohio were clapping. We were there for a state writing competition. My English teacher told me to stand.

I looked around, confused. The cuts on my forearms itched against my peach sweater. No one knew about the cuts. My teacher repeated for me to stand.

"You won first place," she said.

I won on the basis of three stories written that same day in timed sessions. The only story I remember: Three girls stand in line for a movie that they have no intention of seeing. They want to be seen. They choose to stand next to a movie poster that shows a car crashed into a tree. Two of them chew gum and talk about boys. The other girl is thinking about her sister who died in a car accident. "Anne wants to lose herself in a movie" is the only sentence I remember. Her sister's name was Annie. I titled the story "i." Nothing much happened beyond that.

As an adult handed me a trophy, I told myself Jeanne won.

SIX

In the story, the *i* appeared in the dead sister's name. But I could be misremembering. If I am misremembering, then my mistake implies that I want, or wanted, to trade places with Jeanne. But that doesn't feel right.

Also, I packed the thought *I told myself Jeanne won* into my memory because it seems like it belongs there, but honestly I don't know if it belongs there. I remember my itchy peach sweater, the applause, the classmates who congratulated me and the classmates who didn't. But I don't have the folder of stories that transformed into a trophy, and I don't have the trophy. Later I received an A- in a science class (I think it was science), and threw away my awards.

Jeanne wasn't always on my mind. I knew my dad loved me. I don't want to imply that Jeanne occupied my whole life. I did things without thinking of her.

Such as?

I need to address that.

I worry that Jeanne and my feelings about Jeanne are entering memories where they never were. I'm tempted to remove her.

I'm also tempted to empty my childhood and adolescence of any signs of sadness or mental illness: the wrist scratching, the foot cutting, the overwhelming speed of thoughts that left me dizzy, the occasional voices. And then how after my dad died they turned angry.

Maybe my grief, or illness, was planted before he died.

My classmates often reminded me, "Your dad is going to die."

And Jeanne died.

Preemptive grieving—is that a thing?

DAD

My friends no longer felt like my friends. They told me to study less because boys don't like to feel inferior to girls. They told me I should get a nose job. I begged my parents to transfer me out of Catholic school. I decided that *feeling like an outsider* and *being told I'm ugly* were not persuasive enough arguments. So I made a list of all the other reasons I hated Catholic school: the math teacher taught more religion than math; some of the boys raised their arms like they were Nazis during the Pledge of Allegiance and the teachers never punished them; one of the nuns asked us to scratch her back during movies. My mom said the public school was in the news practically every day because of drugs.

"That's because the Catholic school doesn't have to report crimes," I told her. "You think Catholic kids don't do drugs?"

"The public school has a metal detector," she said, probably shouted.

"Isn't a metal detector a good thing?" I asked, probably shouted.

My dad played the more sensible role—in front of me, at least. He and I visited the public school, spoke with a guidance counselor and the principal, observed an English honors class.

Impressed, he helped present my case to my mom. What convinced her was a simple detail.

"A kid with green hair held open the door for me," he told her. "Not once, in all the years Jeannie went to Catholic school, did a kid hold open a door for me."

JEANNE

It was my first day of high school. No one at the public school knew me. During attendance, teachers called me Barbara, and each time I asked that they call me Jeannie.

"Why Jeannie?" one of them asked.

"It's a long story," I said.

"J-E-A-N-N-E?" another asked.

"There's an *i*," I said.

DAD

I founded and edited the school newspaper. My GPA ranked above a 4.0. I was president of several clubs.

But I spent less and less time with my dad, who no longer could climb the stairs. Now he and my mom slept on the foldout sofa in the living room.

My friends thought I was lucky: the entire second floor to myself.

But I didn't like it. When I was a girl, my bed mirrored my parents' bed—separated by a wall. If I couldn't sleep, I'd knock three times on the wall, and my dad would knock back.

JEANNE

A black-and-white video played on an old television in a small dark room of the driving school. About a dozen other unlicensed teenagers watched. I heard sirens and closed my eyes.

"You, open your eyes," the instructor said to me.

On the screen, a man was hunched over his wheel, blood all over. He was a trucker who'd drifted asleep while driving. He was dead now, the video's narrator said. The screen then cut to an interview with his wife. She said she'd have to work harder now, pay for her children's education on her own. Her tone sounded cold, annoyed. Was she an actor? Grieving in her own way? Maybe her tears had been edited out.

My mom kept a precise log of my driving hours. She marked the date and time of each drive.

"Your mom actually does that?" a friend asked me.

The state of Ohio abided by the honor code. After completing the required fifty hours, I registered for the written test. I'd just turned sixteen. I couldn't die in a car accident at sixteen, as Jeanne did. My dad would blame himself.

"You'll do fine," my mom said as she dropped me off at the Bureau of Motor Vehicles.

One question asked how to maintain a safe following distance. I wondered about the distance between the car Jeanne had been in and the car ahead of her. In my mind I went on to connect every question to Jeanne. I chose answers quickly. I just wanted the test to end.

"I failed it," I told my mom on the ride home.

"It's okay," my mom assured me when the test results arrived in the mail. "You can take it again."

"Don't tell Dad."

"He won't be angry. Why would he be angry?"

Jeanne.

I took the test again and passed with a perfect score.

MENTAL ILLNESS

Soon after I turned sixteen, the voice returned. Again, *Jeanne*, or maybe *Jeannie*. And again, on our staircase. Only this time it echoed. I gripped the blue railing and it felt loose. I began to climb and with each step the voice grew louder. I never thought I'd hear it again. The voice, though—something was missing, or something it was saying was missing something from it.

I went downstairs and took my keys. I told my parents that I was driving to the mall, or to a friend's house, anywhere within our town's borders—I forget. My parents wanted me to drive in town for at least a few months before setting out alone. I'd just received my driver's license. But I needed to leave.

I nervously drove two and a half hours to an art museum. I stayed in my lane, afraid to pass the slow-moving car ahead of me. The trip should have taken maybe half the time.

I reached the museum and the quietness inside, which I thought would calm me, only emphasized my loud thoughts as I walked from gallery to gallery. I stopped when I noticed a small group of men and women clustered around a painting. A tour guide was describing the life of Vincent van Gogh.

The guide said that the artist's brother Vincent was born, and died, March 30, 1852. The artist was born March 30, 1853. Every Sunday as a child, Van Gogh passed his brother's marked grave as he entered the church where their father, Theodorus, preached. Whether the knowledge affected Van Gogh—that he shared both his name and birthday with a dead sibling—remained unknown, the guide said.

I went to the painting. A white house with a blue-tiled roof appeared in the center. A long stone wall climbed the canvas as my eyes skimmed the loose brushstrokes from left to right. The blue-gray sky didn't look sad in the way that I thought a blue-gray sky would.

MOM

By my junior year, my dad could barely walk without a cane. Rather than use the wheelchair strung up in our garage rafters, he stayed at home and watched the news. He no longer could read. His tools in the garage gathered dust.

By my senior year, I realized that I might leave him.

I could take a year off, I told my parents. What did one year matter?

"Even if you went to community college," my mom said, "you'd still be too far away. Do you understand?"

The schools I applied to were in Massachusetts, Illinois, Ohio, and New York.

•

"He didn't want you in New York," my mom tells me, "but he wouldn't tell you no. I had to talk you out of it. You didn't know this, but after you told him you were applying there, he went in the bathroom and threw up."

"I was so mad at you," I say.

"Yeah, you yelled at me, told me I didn't understand and that you'd go anyway. You took your car keys and drove to a friend's house. But you came home an hour later and apologized. He hated to hear us fight."

"We didn't fight that much," I say.

"But when we did. Don't get me wrong, it was the usual teen-age stuff. It had to do with a curfew or you going out of town with a friend. I don't know, small stuff. I couldn't even tell you what. The only time I remember your father raising his voice with you was when you and me were arguing about something. You were in high school. He couldn't walk anymore, not without his cane. He got on his hands and knees and crawled up those stairs. You were standing at the top. He said, 'I want you to respect your mother.' Well then you lost it. You cried. You apologized. I think you cared so much about being perfect for him."

DAD

My parents were downstairs, discussing our house. I eavesdropped through the grate in my bedroom floor.

"We might get $50,000," my mom said.

"How much would that cover?" my dad asked.

"I don't know," she said. "A year at a private college."

Where would they go?

I applied for every scholarship I could.

•

The day the World Trade Center fell, I turned off the news and asked my dad to play poker at the kitchen table. I wanted the towers to stop falling.

"I was thinking," I said. "Maybe I delay college, take a year off."

He shook his head no.

"But I don't want to leave you," I said.

"College is important."

"Well I won't go to school in New York. Not after what happened there."

I didn't say, *Not after what happened there today.* I thought, *Not after what happened there to Jeanne.*

•

One afternoon, I was in a computer room at the high school, editing the newspaper. As my advisor leaned next to me and stared at the computer screen, he put his hand on my thigh. His hand felt oddly heavy, looked absurdly white against my tan legs.

"I like it," he said, pointing—with his other hand—at a new font I'd chosen.

The hand on my thigh moved higher and higher. I was wearing shorts.

"What do you think?" he said.

When the hand moved between my legs, I stood.

"I need to use the bathroom," I said.

I left, washed my face with cold water. I told myself that what happened hadn't happened, or hadn't happened enough to be discussed.

•

I asked my mom if I could spend the rest of the school year at home.

"I want to be here with Dad," I said.

"Something else is wrong," she said.

I hesitated. I was surrounded by photographs of myself. Our downstairs looked like a shrine to me. If my dad learned about my advisor, would he regret having let me transfer out of the Catholic school? Would he be mad at me for hiding this from him?

"You can't tell Dad."

"Tell him what?" she said.

I told her, and she left the room.

"Don't," I insisted.

But there he was, in his blue pajama pants and gray sweatshirt, what he often wore those days. She helped him sit in the chair across from me. His cane was propped against it.

"Tell your father," she said.

I avoided his eyes.

"It's a teacher," I told him.

My dad's hand clenched his cane.

"What did he do?" he asked.

I began to cry.

"He touched her," my mom said.

My teacher touching me was less important than my dad hearing that my teacher touched me.

"If only I were well enough," my dad told the floor.

•

The principal looked at my mom, then at me. I could feel the hot tears. The principal closed the door. My mom sat beside me.

"Tell him," my mom said.

I tried to give examples—my advisor's tone of voice, the expression in his eyes, the invitations to his place, but when said aloud, the details sounded inconsequential.

"He touched her," my mom said. "If my husband were in better health, that teacher would be under a fresh sidewalk."

The principal said he believed me. He assured me of it.

The detectives did not.

They met with me several times.

They said I looked tired. I said I had trouble sleeping. They asked if I thought my ability to reason had been compromised by a lack of sleep.

•

I read my acceptance letter—from the university I most wanted to attend. A six-hour drive away, right outside Chicago, it offered me almost a full ride and by the last month of high school, I had college entirely paid for through scholarships and grants. My parents wouldn't have to sell the house.

"Tuition, books, living expenses, everything," I told them.

My dad squeezed my hand.

"You," he said, smiling.

"She got the brains from you," my mom said.

I soon learned that my advisor also would be leaving town. A school elsewhere in Ohio had offered him a position. There wasn't enough proof to take away his teaching license.

"I'm sorry," my principal said. "It's the best I could do."

•

My dad tried to renew his driver's license the last year of his life. My mom told me the story.

The woman at the Bureau of Motor Vehicles asked him how tall he was as she measured him. He straightened his back as best he could.

"Five feet, ten inches," he answered.

By then he was my height, five feet, six inches. The woman looked at my mom and smiled.

"You're exactly right," the woman told him.

My dad smiled for the camera. He was wearing his glasses and a blue dress shirt. His narrowed eyes and the cheek shadows bore a down-dragging gravity. The printed ID listed his height as five feet, ten inches. Below that an image of the state flag appeared. Overlapping the flag: NONDRIVER.

The woman told him he could sit while she printed it.

"It won't take long," she said.

He held my mom's hand while they waited.

When it was done, the woman handed him the card.

"I can drive then?" my dad asked.

She looked at my mom. My mom nodded yes.

"You're all set," the woman said.

He thanked her, and then, to my mom: "Maybe you should drive us home."

•

The day of my high school graduation, my mom gently told me my dad would stay home.

"It's too hot outside," she explained. "I don't think it'd be a good idea."

"Then I don't want to go," I told her.

"No," my dad said. "This is an important day."

He watched me accept my diploma on the public access channel.

After the ceremony, at home, I again proposed staying in town for another year.

He shook his head no.

"I want to be with you," I said.

"This is what he wants," my mom said.

The day I left town, I told him that I wanted to stay.

"Tell me not to leave," I told him.

He squeezed my hand and said nothing.

SEVEN

Here, above my desk, hang four black-and-white photos of my dad as a young man in New York. His thick dark hair is brushed back, a slight wave to it. He is thin with large dark eyes, a wide smile, and a strong jaw.

"He looks like a movie star in these pictures," I tell my mom.

"You have his eyes," she says. "You look like him."

In every photo he wears a tie and slacks, which seem almost absurd against the modest scenery: dry overgrown grass, an A-frame house, a rope swing with two crude wooden seats. Two of the photos he dated July 6, 1945 (I recognize his perfect cursive), a day that, according to the *Farmer's Almanac*, was foggy with light rain and thunder. But the sky looks clear, or as clear as a black-and-white photo allows. In a year his mother, Josephine, would die in her sleep at fifty-four of gout, and Jeanne would be born. He smiled that July day with his arms around his two sisters, Anna and Mary, in their floral aprons. And in the other dated photo, his mother stands in a pale button-down collared dress between him and Anna's husband, Tony. Mary, Anna, and Tony visited us when I was a child, but they never mentioned my dad's life before me. His brother, Frank, and their father aren't photographed.

"Frank was shy," my mom says. "He and your dad were very close, but your dad and his father had a difficult relationship."

The undated photos remain more mysterious. In one he kneels on the grass with a small mutt between his hands, and in the other photo he kneels between a boy and girl in denim over-alls on rope swings. Who are those children? What was the name of that mutt? I asked him once and now I forget.

What if I look at Jeanne as an illness? As a diagnosis? Does that sound bad?

As bad as calling her a narrative device? As bad as calling her a metaphor?

Metaphors. I should make a list of metaphors because metaphors reveal complicated emotions. I once kept a journal where under-neath each date was a metaphor. I never actually detailed what happened. I simply made up metaphors that encapsulated my general impressions/feelings about a particular occurrence. For example: an overturned boat kept appearing in entries dated April 2003. May was unlit windows. My dad would have turned eighty-one years old. He'd have turned six months dead.

DAD

The first day of my sociology class, the professor distributed an anonymous survey to the students. Most of my classes were fifteen students. This class, however, was the largest on campus, six hundred students. One of my journalism classmates sat next to me in the lecture hall. I still remember her. Her father practiced law in Chicago. She wanted to edit a fashion magazine. She rotated her designer bags on a daily schedule. One question asked us to circle our family's annual income. I circled "less than $20,000."

"Do you not have a family?" she asked loudly.

Faces in the large lecture hall turned to look. I slunk down in my seat.

After class, she asked how I was there.

"What do you mean?"

"Are you on a scholarship or something?"

"Yes."

"Are your parents alive?"

"Yes," I said, unable to look her in the eyes.

•

One Friday night, less than a month after I started college, I went with my roommate to visit her parents' home in Chicago. For whatever reason, I left my cell phone on my bed.

On the drive back to campus on Sunday, I looked out the car window and noticed two women who looked identical to my mom and her friend Sharon. *Homesick*, I told myself. *You miss your parents.* My roommate dropped me off at our dorm, and she went to her boyfriend's dorm. When I went into our room, my phone was blinking. I knew. I threw on my sneakers and ran toward where I'd seen my mom and Sharon. As I ran, I pressed the phone against my ear, listening to the messages.

"I'm on my way to you," my mom said in the first message.

Next message: "Where are you? They won't let me into your dorm."

Next message: "Jeannie, call me as soon as you get this."

She knew that I spent most of my time at the library, so I ran there, and found her and Sharon, their backs facing me, underneath a tree. I stopped running.

"Where's Dad?" I said.

My mom turned and hugged me. She said he was at home, and hospice was caring for him. Someone was caring for him, my thinking went, which meant he'd be fine.

As we walked back toward my dorm, she explained that she'd tried to find me there, but the student in the mail room had refused to let her in.

"Did you tell him about Dad?"

Even though she told him that my dad was dying, that she'd driven six hours in the middle of the night to tell me in person, and that she couldn't reach me on my phone, the student said letting her into the hallway would violate university rules.

I ignored the word "dying." Or maybe she never used it. Maybe she said "not well." Maybe she said "very sick." Maybe, like me, she was in denial.

When we reached my dorm, I told her to wait in the car with Sharon. I avoided looking at the mail room, went into my room and packed, then decided to deal with the student.

I reached my right arm through the open mail room window and gripped his neck. I remembered my dad reaching his arm through the driver's open window.

"You'd be worth getting expelled for," I said.

The student looked surprised, then frightened.

"Do you remember a blonde woman who came in here looking for her daughter?"

The student nodded.

"Do you want to guess who I am?"

Right then a woman with a white sweater tied around her shoulders walked by with presumably her husband and their son, another resident in my dorm. It was parents' weekend.

"Everyone here is just so friendly," she said.

Then she registered the scene.

"Oh. We should—"

Her voice dropped off. I loosened my grip.

"From now on, if you see me," I said, "I want you to look away. I want to forget you exist."

I walked outside with my bags. The air was fresh, the sky was clear, but my dad was dying.

•

When he began dying, men built a wall around his dying. They installed a door. My mom said this was for his privacy.

He was dying in what used to be the living room.

He was dying between the silver rails of a borrowed bed.

He was dying.

I fell to my knees and pressed my head into the carpet.

"No, no, no," I repeated.

I stood and squeezed my dad's hands.

"I didn't know, Dad. Please know that. I didn't know."

•

A hospice nurse introduced herself. I remember she wore her glasses on a ribbon. They hung half-mast against her chest.

She demonstrated how to administer the morphine, how to turn him.

"He needs to be turned over every few hours. Otherwise he'll develop bedsores."

She showed me his bedpan.

"We'll do most of this," she explained, "but there may be times you'll have to do this."

"The morphine?" I asked.

She touched me lightly on the shoulder.

"Don't you worry," she said. "You'll have a lot of help."

MOM

"Did your dad say anything to you," my mom asks, "when you came home from college?"

"It seemed like it hurt him to speak," I tell her. "He mostly squeezed my hand. Why?"

"He was very angry with me for calling you."

"He didn't want me there?"

"It was a matter of pride. He didn't want you to see him like that. He told me not to take you away from school. He said to wait to call you until he was buried. I told him, 'Terry, I can't do that.' He didn't want me to call his other daughters either, but Sharon told him, 'Terry, your other girls could come after Barb for not calling. They could blame her.' He said, 'Call them.' I hated going against him. But I didn't think it'd be right otherwise. After I brought you home, he gave me a look. He was mad at me, I think."

He didn't want to see me; or rather, he didn't want me to see him like that. I try to understand. I need to understand.

"I'm sure he understood," I say.

•

When my mom called his other daughters to tell them he was dying, did she say "dying"? Maybe she said "dying." "Close to the end," maybe? I told myself he wasn't dying.

When they arrived with their dark hair and dark eyes and dark clothes, they looked strikingly sophisticated. One of them held a box of chocolates.

"He can't eat them, can he?" she asked me nervously.

I took her to be Carol.

"I don't think so," I said.

"Is he?" she began.

"He might be able to eat them," I said. "Let's hold on to them."

Them, him. I meant hold on to him.

DAD

I sat by the railroad tracks and watched a freight train rush by.

I circled the block.

I circled the block some more.

I'd left the house to give his other daughters time alone with him. I remember looking at my watch. I forget how much time had passed, if it seemed like the right amount of time, not enough time, too much time.

I meandered downtown, to the lakefront where my parents and I fed seagulls when I was a child. Roller coasters rose like soft cursive in the gray distance.

I walked home.

When I opened the front door, Debbie was trimming his hair in the kitchen. A blue bath towel was draped around his shoulders. His head was bent over our green-and-white checkered tablecloth. Arlene photographed the scene, among other scenes from their visit, and later mailed me the photos. Only now do I see how old he was: his olive coloring had been wrung out of his face—much thinner than I remember—and his shoulders were gently stooped forward.

But back then I didn't notice. He didn't look old, not to me. He simply looked like my dad.

•

Somehow the subject of his name arose.

"Terry is your name," one of his daughters told him; which one, I forget.

"Giovanni is his name," I said. "He goes by Terry."

They looked at one another.

He nodded.

"His father's barbershop was called Terry's Barbershop when he bought it," I said. "Rather than change the sign, his father changed his own name from Giovanni to Terry. If a form required him to give a middle name, he wrote 'John.' He thought an American name would help business. So then Dad started getting called Terry."

Surely they knew stories unfamiliar to me.

That evening Carol told me, "You had more time with him than we did."

•

My mom drove to the grocery store. I went for another aimless walk that was either too long or not long enough. Carol, Arlene, and Debbie stayed behind.

When I returned home, a stranger's car was parked in the driveway. I ran inside. A man's voice that wasn't my dad's was in my dad's room. I rushed to his doorway and found his other daughters and a priest holding hands and praying around him. I went to the back porch and sat on the rusted aluminum glider with my dog, Gigi.

"He didn't want a priest," I told Gigi. "He said that. No priest."

My dad was Catholic but he was private.

And yet here he is.

•

Jeanne's sisters were leaving.

We must have hugged.

Surely we hugged.

I can't summon an image of us hugging.

•

I quietly read *Hamlet* beside his bed while he slept.

"He was a man, take him for all in all," Hamlet says of his dead father. "I shall not look upon his like again."

My dad squeezed my hand. I squeezed back harder.

My mom put her hands on my shoulders. I followed her into the front room and listened to her explain that I'd need to leave soon.

"Your father wants you back at school," she said. "You've already missed a week of classes."

"But I want to be here."

"You can come home on weekends."

I insisted I stay. She insisted I leave. She called Amtrak. I would be leaving in just a few days.

"It's what your father wants," she said.

JEANNE

When my dad was dying, did he see Jeanne?

I remember thinking: *Please let there be somewhere where she is, so that—if he has to die (but not now, please not now)—she can be there, too.*

Yet I don't remember what I felt, or rather: there weren't words for it. I experienced his dying how a child must experience a storm before knowing the vocabulary surrounding it—not just the word "storm" but "sky" and "lightning" and "thunder" and "rain" and whatever else. My dad's dying was a terrifying experience, but "terrifying" is insufficient. The language of death ("illness," "cancer," "mortality") does little to describe it, explain it, justify it, which is why I resort to metaphor.

I remember standing outside the room where his body was failing, a scream locked inside me. I'd fallen down a cool black well—and no one was coming for me, because I wouldn't make a sound.

DAD

My mom and I were in the room with him. She was holding his hand. He motioned me closer and said something.

"What did you say, Dad?"

His voice was almost gone. He repeated his words. I looked at my mom.

"He said, 'You're beautiful,'" my mom told me.

The last thing he said to my mom: "You're my best friend."

For the next two days, my dad said nothing. I said everything I could. I made promises while his hospice nurses moved in and out.

I taped photographs from my childhood along the silver rails of the bed: my dad reading a book to me despite the white patch over his eye; my dad pulling me in a wooden sled; my dad clutching me on his lap and looking off somewhere as if he knew this was coming.

JEANNE

A light lit up the window, and I heard a car park in our driveway. My boyfriend let himself into the house. He went to a college more than two hours away. I'd been a high school freshman when he was a high school senior. We shared almost no common interests. Each time I tried to break off our relationship, he reminded me that my dad liked him, and didn't I want to be with someone my dad liked? I reasoned that I had to see my boyfriend only on weekends and summers. It sounds cold to say this: he hasn't seemed relevant to the narrative until now.

My boyfriend asked if I would have dinner with him. It was a Friday night. Saturday would be my last full day with my dad. I clenched my dad's hand.

"I want to be here," I said.

My boyfriend left the room and returned with my mom.

"Go on," she said. "Your father's sleeping."

I put on my coat and followed my boyfriend to his car. He played with the radio as we drove up the main road in town.

"I'm not hungry," I said. "Can you take me home?"

He asked when I last ate. I asked him to stop fooling with the radio. He said I needed to eat.

"My father is sick."

"That doesn't mean you stop eating. Where do you want to go?"

I said one restaurant. He insisted on another.

"Then why did you even ask?" I said.

"Are you wearing your seat belt?"

I looked up at the yellow traffic light. I glanced in the side mirror. He braked. The small reflection of a car behind us grew and disappeared.

I remember sirens next. Then two EMTs helping me out of my seat.

"I shouldn't have left him," I said.

"He's standing right here," an EMT replied, not understanding I meant my dad.

The EMTs helped me into the ambulance. My boyfriend rode in the back and held my hand.

"Jeanne died in a car accident," I told him.

"Her name is Jeannie," he informed the EMTs.

The EMTs assured me I'd be fine.

"My father is dying, and I'm not with him."

MOM

I didn't want my parents to know I'd been in a car accident. I gave the nurses a fake phone number, and my boyfriend's grandparents handled the paperwork.

When I arrived home from the hospital a few hours later, my mom was on the floor next to his bed, tossing and turning and crying in her sleep. (He'd requested a bigger bed from hospice—"Where's my wife going to sleep? You need to bring a bigger bed"—but my mom told him it'd be okay. Every night she pretended to sleep next to him until he fell asleep. Then she moved to the floor.) Gigi, twelve years old by then, slept underneath his bed. I went upstairs to my own, pulled my blankets over my head, and invented a story: the earth had swallowed our house, and now my parents, Gigi, and I lived together in an underground world.

DAD

The room was dark. It was the middle of the night. I told my dad I was leaving.

"Mom says it's what you want, and so it's what I'm doing."

He said nothing, could say nothing. His voice was gone.

I kissed his forehead. I told him what time my train would arrive in Chicago. I told him I'd be home the next weekend. I told him that I didn't want to leave him, but that I was leaving for him.

I promised I would write a book for him.

MOM

I loaded my suitcase into the car and tried to hold back tears. My mom drove. I didn't say much. I didn't know what to say. As we approached the train depot, she pointed to an old white-sided, two-story house. Its windows were boarded, and a TO BE CONDEMNED sign was posted on the front door. She let out a big sigh.

"No real surprise. They never took care of nothing."

I understood then that she'd pointed to her parents' home. I never could remember which one it was. I remembered a story she'd told me. Her mother had thrown a butcher knife at her when she was twelve. The knife just missed. My mom picked it up, threw it back at her, and ran. Another time her mother threw a metal rake at her. My mom still has a scar over her left eye. Her father was mostly gone.

"Never should have had kids," she said of her parents.

My mom spent most of her childhood at her maternal great-grandmother's house, also somewhere around the train depot.

She pulled into the depot lot and parked.

"I don't want to leave," I said.

My mom stared ahead at the empty tracks.

"Your father wants you back at school. I do, too. You're so smart."

I looked back at her childhood home.

"Sure don't take after me," she said.

The train whistled from somewhere in the distance. I went outside toward the tracks. Its light appeared. When I turned around, my mom was at the nose of our car with my suitcase.

"I love you," she said, holding me tight.

She was shaking.

"I love you, too," I said.

"I'll be home next weekend," I said. "Remind Dad."

DAD

On the train, I couldn't sleep. No one sat next to me, probably because I was crying. I looked at photographs of my dad, and invented metaphors and similes in my journal: "The scratches in the train window look like overgrown weeds. Today is a locked window—no, a bombed-out landscape, an empty landscape. Today is dirt. Today is a broken glass floor. Today is a trapdoor I could fall through at any time." The train ride took six hours, as expected. I left Chicago's Union Station and hailed a cab back to campus rather than taking public transportation. My mom had insisted I do this.

"My father drove a cab when he was young," I told the driver. "In New York."

I spent the rest of the drive talking about my dad. I never mentioned he was dying.

The driver parked in front of my dorm. I imagined my dad behind the wheel, and tipped the driver what must have been a generous amount. He thanked me twice.

After I entered my dorm, I realized I'd forgotten the keys to both my hall door and room. I called my dorm phone from my cell, but my roommate didn't answer. She must be at her boyfriend's, I thought. So I called the resident assistant on duty. She asked for ten dollars to unlock my room, which was standard practice. I searched through my purse and realized I'd lost my wallet. I handed her the only money I had: seven dollars and some change out of my pocket.

"I might have more in my room."

"It's all right," she said.

I dropped my bags in the middle of my room and sat on the floor next to them, anxious about what to do next. It was a Sunday. I could go to the library, catch up on schoolwork, but I didn't want to see anyone and I didn't want to be seen. I called home, but no one answered. I called my boyfriend and told him I'd left my keys at home.

"I'm on my way," he said.

"You don't have to drive them here. You can mail them."

"Your father died this morning."

How easily he said it.

"Jeannie?"

I curled up on my floor, hugged my knees, and screamed.

EIGHT

My mom recently gave me a piece of the library's glass floor. I use it as a paperweight for recent drafts of *My Father's Glass Eye*.

The year before my dad died, the library was renovated. The glass floor was removed.

The year my dad died, the floor was cut into three hundred rectangular pieces—just four inches by three inches each. There must have been floor left, but I don't know what happened to it.

The year after my dad died, the three hundred pieces were polished and sold to benefit the library.

I spend my nights researching such things.

MOM

My dad died at the same time my train was pulling into Chicago's Union Station. The detail seems symbolic. I call my mom, mention it.

"I didn't know what to do," she says. "You were back at school, and I didn't want to tell you over the phone, and I couldn't drive to get you. I was a mess."

She called my then boyfriend.

"I told him that I wanted you to hear it in person. He wasn't supposed to tell you on the phone."

MENTAL ILLNESS

My boyfriend and his grandparents picked me up at my dorm in the early afternoon.

I sat in the backseat with my boyfriend. His grandfather drove. His grandmother tried to make conversation.

"The drive," she said, "was no big deal. Just six hours."

My dad died six hours after I left him.

I couldn't follow the rest of what she said. My thoughts moved so fast they seemed motionless: *I left, his left eye, I left his left eye, he is not his glass eye, it was not even glass, the i left him.*

MOM

The thick stench of my dad's cologne filled the house. My mom came to the door and hugged me.

"Be careful of glass," she said and began to pace. "I think I cleaned up most of it."

She'd smashed his bottles of cologne and aftershave. I imagined pieces of his glass eye everywhere. It wasn't even made of glass; I knew this.

"I didn't want anyone else to have it," she explained.

I looked inside the living room. The bed was empty. When I turned around, I noticed she was wearing one of his shirts.

"I told him I was going upstairs. I went upstairs to change the sheets on your bed. When I came back down—"

DAD

My first night home, I kept knocking on the wall.

"Come on, Dad," I kept saying.

His doctors often told me when I was a girl, "You keep him young." So it stands to reason, if I'd spent more time with him in high school, he wouldn't have died—at least not when he did. He would've lived longer. He'd still be alive.

Come on, Dad.

MOM

The next morning, the funeral director came to our house. It still reeked of my dad's cologne. The director pretended not to notice. He sat between my mom and me on our couch, paging through a catalogue of caskets. Several featured "airtight" locks.

"I don't know," my mom said, staring blankly at the catalogue.

Gigi walked into the room, left the room, returned. She looked lost. At night she'd dig at the carpet where my dad's bed had been.

"Your dog looks rather old," the funeral director said.

"My husband loved that dog."

"You know, we often bury people with their pets," he said.

"I couldn't," my mom said, looking at me.

She left the room. I remembered something she once told me about my dad; he'd been so devastated by Jeanne's death that his brother, Frank, had to pick out the flowers and casket.

"The bare minimum," I said. "My father would want the bare minimum."

"I'm only showing you the options."

My mom returned. She told the funeral director she would like to begin paying for her funeral.

"This way," she said, "it will make things easier on my daughter here."

·

I needed a dress for the funeral.

My mom drove me to a department store where before us shirts, suits, slacks, and ties hung from floor to ceiling. I imagined buying these clothes and replacing them with those in his closet. My mom would no longer wear his shirts and not know that she had, in some small way, moved on.

We found our way to the dresses and combed through everything black, feeling the fabric on the round racks but never settling. A saleswoman showed me a short black dress, its straps flirtatiously thin and off the shoulder. I wanted my mom to say: *My daughter wants a longer dress, something no higher than the knee, preferably the shin.*

"Her father died," she said.

After finding a long-sleeved, modest black dress, we drove home.

On the way there, my mom told me what she wanted to wear to her own funeral: the beige dress she married my dad in.

"You'll find it in the garage," she said, "in the back closet."

She pulled into our driveway and I ran into the house. Later I found her in the garage, rearranging clothes hanging from a metal rod. A brown vinyl shower curtain protected them from dust.

"Here it is," she said. "This is the dress."

•

Of course it was hard for my mom. She lost the man she loved.

Sometimes I forget my given name: Barbara, from the Greek *barbaros*, meaning "foreign" or "strange," "traveler from a foreign land."

My birth certificate, my high school and university diplomas, my lease, the labels on my prescription drugs—I feel as if they belong to someone else.

Sometimes I forget I share a name with my mom.

We share so few qualities. She has blonde hair and blue eyes. I have brown hair and brown eyes.

"You're just like your father," she says. "You're a perfectionist, like him. He'd get all worked up over nothing."

She knows how to relax, couldn't care less about what others think.

She tells me a story. After she and my dad married, he moved into the small saltbox house where she lived, the house where they'd raise me. One morning, my dad woke early and rearranged all the canned goods in the pantry. He put the soups with the soups, the beans with the beans, and so on.

"I think he even alphabetized them," my mom says.

Then he went outside to the garage, and my mom—just to tease him—took them out of order.

"He was so upset at first," my mom says. "I told him, 'What's the big deal? Does it really matter?' And he said, 'You're right. I guess not.'

"You know," she continues, "he hadn't worn a pair of jeans in his life until he married me. Almost sixty years and not one pair of jeans. He was always dressed classy. I remember this one night we were out dancing. We went out dancing every Friday before you were born. His legs were better then. He was an excellent dancer. People would stop and watch us. Anyway, we were dancing and I started laughing. He said, 'What's so funny?' I pointed out that he had one navy blue shoe on and one black shoe. Well, that was that. We had to drive home so he could change."

DAD

He was in his casket, looking like no one I knew. I'd been carrying his glasses with me. I slid them on his face.

"That looks more like him," my mom said.

But that wasn't what I wanted; I wanted him to see me.

"Would you like to keep your father's glass eye?" the funeral director asked.

I looked at my dad, his eyes glued shut.

"No," I said. "I couldn't."

MOM

As we sat in the front row before my dad's body, she stood and threw herself over the casket.

Someone pulled her back.

And when she sat next to me, I held her shaking hand.

And when the priest asked if anyone had any words to say, I said nothing. No one said anything.

Only a handful of people were in the room.

Two of the pallbearers were strangers.

My dad hadn't wanted a funeral, but the priest had told my mom that I deserved to see my dad one last time. She invited almost no one. His other daughters decided not to come.

The ceremony was for me.

"That's not your father in there," she said as the polished hearse doors closed.

It was a body, its eyes glued shut.

I'd never see them again.

DAD

Where did the men take him?

I was told the hard November ground needed to break before they could bury my dad.

So where was he?

PART TWO

NINE

After my dad died, time rearranged itself. I understood it only in relation to his death.

The Memory Game might be the solution, the overarching metaphor for the book. The Memory Game can hold the eye. But he's not his eye.

So is this the plot? Is the narrative present the arc that contains the plot? And then the past just sits there? Or am I supposed to find an arc within the past? My dad's dying, should that be in the present tense—as a means of indicating he's always dying? But what's the intention there?

The future tense, can something be done with that?

DAD

After his funeral, I sorted through a small wooden box that belonged to him. I'd never seen it before. I thought that maybe it held a photograph of Jeanne. Instead I found divorce papers.

"Dad was married to a woman named Mercedes?" I asked.

"He didn't want you to know," my mom explained. "They weren't together more than a month."

"Mercedes?"

"He told me he was drunk. He didn't know what he was doing when he was drunk. It was after Jeanne died. He really lost it after that. He drank to forget, I think. When I met him, he was a big drinker. All that stopped after we had you."

"Why would he think I'd care about Mercedes?"

"Your old Catholics don't believe in divorce. He was ashamed."

A week later, I returned to college with a sentence trapped in my thoughts: "After Jeanne died, he really lost it."

•

Back at college, I spent more time with the maintenance man in my dorm than I did with the other students. He and I communicated with hand motions, as he spoke almost no English and

I spoke almost no Spanish. One morning in the laundry room, he explained that he'd been a doctor in Mexico. He made more money in the United States, cleaning up after college students, than he did healing patients in his hometown. He mailed his earnings to his wife and daughter, both in Mexico.

"Su padre?" he asked me.

I knew the word for it.

"Muerto," I answered.

How easy it was to say in another language.

"Su madre?" the maintenance man asked.

How do you say: *Seems dead*?

MENTAL ILLNESS

In the weeks after my dad died, I tied nooses, cut my feet, scratched my wrists. I wandered through campus with my phone pressed against my ear, telling my dad that "I should have been with you."

Alone in my dorm room one night, I was at my desk, writing to him, when the lights flashed off. Then on. Off. On.

The walls approached me from all sides.

"I'm sorry," I said, closing my eyes.

My chair legs screeched. I was being pushed or dragged; I didn't know.

"I'm sorry," I repeated.

I opened my eyes, and I was where I had been before I closed them: at my desk, an unfinished letter to my dad in front of me.

That night I wrote in the margins of my textbooks: "I left him." Over and over: "I left him. Jeanne would not have left him."

MOM

I returned to Ohio to spend Christmas with my mom. The staircase had no gold garland wrapped around it. No stuffed Santas sat between its balusters. There were no nativities, no wreaths. There was no tree, no Dad.

"It's not the same without him," my mom said.

I looked around for some sign of him. His work shoes sat with a pile of other shoes and boots near the back door. His cane hung from our coatrack.

"I'm going to stop at the store to get some shampoo," I lied.

"I have shampoo," she said. "So much of it."

"I use a new kind."

DAD

I drove to the downtown harbor, where signs of Christmas were everywhere: red ribbons fastened to streetlamps, green garland wrapped around the railings of the boathouses, pine trees dressed in ornaments and fat blinking bulbs of light. I parked the car outside the barbershop where my dad took me after he no longer could cut my hair. A young man and woman walked by, pushing a stroller.

"I'm glad you were older when I was born," I said with the windows rolled up.

I reversed and without thinking drove to the local police precinct.

"I need police records for a case I was involved in," I said. "It involved a high school teacher of mine."

I found it surprisingly easy to secure the records.

I drove with them to the cemetery. I parked and with the engine running began reading the detectives' reports. Much of the material was blacked out. My newspaper advisor told the detectives that I hadn't been sleeping. The detectives noted my "bloodshot eyes." They emphasized that I'd waited months to report the "alleged incident." The high school girl in that report didn't know precisely how far up her teacher's hand had wandered. She was reluctant to demonstrate it on her own thigh for the detectives. I left the records in the car and decided to search for my dad's grave, but I couldn't find it underneath all the snow. In the pale yellow sunlight, the cemetery was a white sheet against a vague horizon. I was too embarrassed to ask the cemetery attendant to help me find my dad. So I knelt and started digging through the snow, but I couldn't find his name. I settled on a grave underneath a tree. He was buried near a tree; that, I knew.

"I love you," I said, maybe to a stranger.

MOM

I returned to college, avoided people when I could. I felt afraid to speak in class. I didn't want to start crying, and nothing except *I miss my father* seemed worth saying.

Arlene phoned to wish me a happy nineteenth birthday.

"I would have sent you a card," she said, "but I worried your mother would have thrown it away."

"My mother would do no such thing," I said and hung up.

My mom asked if I'd heard from Arlene on my birthday.

"I did," I said.

"How is she?"

"I don't know. I hung up before asking."

As I explained the exchange to my mom, I thought: *Why am I telling her this?*

"Why does she think I'd do that?" my mom said. "Of course I would never do that."

"I don't know," I said.

"I would never do that."

"That's what I told her," I said.

"She put me through hell after your father died," my mom told me. "You don't know what I went through. She said I was sending him to hell for not having the funeral in a church."

•

I call my mom, ask her to remind me what Arlene said exactly.

"It was so long ago," my mom says.

"But you remember."

"I remember. She said, 'You're baptized in a church, you're married in a church, you die in a church.' Your father didn't want a funeral, period. I did it for you. I tried to explain that to Arlene. But she was upset. I was upset, too. So I went to the priest. He told me, 'I've never heard of something so stupid. You tell her to call me.' Well, she called the priest, and the priest told her off. Look, I know Arlene lost her father. I know that. I know it wasn't easy for her to have her father remarry, especially me—my being so much younger. But it's not like I broke up his first marriage. He and her mother had been long divorced. And it's not like I married your dad for money. I had more than he did when we met, and that's not saying much."

"You loved him," I say. "Arlene loved him. We all did."

"What I wouldn't give to have him back. I was a wreck after he died." She pauses. "I wasn't really there for you after he died."

"You were."

"No, I wasn't."

•

The summer after my dad died, I returned home to see my mom. She looked thin and pale. Even in the heat, she wore all black.

"Where's the fence?" I asked her.

Instead of asking how she was, I asked again, "Where's the fence?"

The fence he built for our driveway—to protect me—was gone.

"It was too much," she said, "having to get out of the car every time to undo it so that I could pull the car in and out."

"What did you do with it?"

"I had to get rid of it. It was falling apart."

"But he made it."

•

It's important to remember, and impossible for me to forget: she lost him too.

I ask her to remind me how she and my dad met.

"We were both working at Providence," she begins.

Providence, which no longer exists, was a hospital in our town.

She organized medical records. He painted the walls. Sometimes they passed one another and smiled—nothing more than that.

"Every afternoon, I'd see him outside my office window, running through the parking lot," she tells me. "He lived across the street. I always wondered why he was in such a hurry."

One day after work, she visited her father in that same hospital. He'd just had surgery. My dad was in the room when she arrived. The two men were chatting about the IAB. Both were Sicilian.

When she came in, my dad said to her, "I didn't know you were Sicilian."

Not long after, they began dating.

On one of their dates, she asked him why he was always running across the parking lot.

"He was embarrassed to tell me," she says. "It was because he watched that soap opera *The Young and the Restless* during his lunch breaks. The show ended just a few minutes before he had to be back to work. He liked the actress Jeanne Cooper. When he told me he wanted to name you after his daughter, I teased him, 'You're naming her after that soap actress.'"

MENTAL ILLNESS

After I returned to campus in the fall, I called my boyfriend. He still lived in Ohio. He was finishing his last semester of college.

"I can't do this anymore," I said.

He asked me what, and I said, "This, us."

He said I missed my dad.

He said, "Why punish me?"

He said, "There's someone else. I knew this would happen."

He demanded a name, an address.

"I'll shoot him," he said. "I swear I'll shoot him."

"I just don't love you," I said.

After we hung up, he called my mom.

"He told me he was worried about you," she explains. "He had me scared. I didn't understand."

He borrowed her car, drove six hours, and yelled at me. I asked him to leave my dorm. There was more yelling, more crying. I screamed, "Get out!" Still in my pajamas, I retreated to the common room, where there was a pool table. No one was there; I'd hoped someone would be. I sat on the table's edge. He grabbed my hand and kept squeezing it. A popular sitcom played on the television next to us.

"Please stop," I said.

He bent down on one knee and proposed marriage with his NCAA Rifle Championship ring. On one side was an engraved image of a shooter crouched with a rifle. On the other side was his last name, a name that he wanted me to take.

"No," I told him.

He led me back into my dorm room and lifted my shirt.

I yanked it back down, but again he lifted it.

"You've lost your mind," he said. "What is that?"

I looked down. I'd written in black marker all over my stomach. The words were indecipherable.

He pulled me by one arm to my mom's car. He drove me to a hospital, but I refused to go inside.

"You need help," he said.

"You need help," I said.

He sighed, drove me to my dorm. He left me with his ring. I tried to give it back.

"Just consider it. I'll buy you a real engagement ring."

I told him no.

"You don't even have to take my name. You can keep Vanasco."

TEN

A manila folder in the top drawer of my desk holds news clippings about my half sisters, articles that I recently found in online newspaper archives.

One article says that among two hundred contestants, Carol won first place in the nationality division of the Catholic Daughters of America's doll contest in 1954; she would have been eleven or twelve.

Another announces Debbie's engagement. In her photograph, her dark hair frames her fine-drawn face. A simple cross hangs from her neck. If she's wearing makeup, it's modest and unnecessary.

The last two articles concern Arlene. Her junior year of high school, she was elected president of the Southeastern Zone of Future Teachers of America. The other article reports that after her high school graduation, she was accepted for stewardess training with the Atlanta Airline School in Hartford, Connecticut.

What would they think if they knew about my research? If they knew how much I cared?

MOM

"Your dad's first wife made his relationship with their girls very difficult," my mom tells me. "During one of their separations, it was his turn to watch Debbie. He was living somewhere else during the separation. Debbie was still a little girl so she was living at their house with her mother. He drove over to pick Debbie up and she ran toward him. Her mother called her back, and Debbie cried. She's real sensitive, like you. After the divorce, his first wife wouldn't talk to them if she found out they were in contact with him. Your dad told me all this. He said he eventually realized he was doing Debbie and her sisters more harm than good by staying. That's why he left New York. It wasn't as if he didn't provide for them. He'd already paid for Carol and Arlene's weddings. He'd soon pay for Debbie's. When I met him, I remember he was going away for a weekend to paint Carol's house. He tried the best he could. But after losing Jeanne, I think that was it for him. He blamed himself. The only reason he didn't kill himself back then, he told me, was on account of his girls. He couldn't do that to them, he said."

DAD

A month after my breakup, I began dating someone new at college. Someone nice, "a gentleman," my dad would have called him. He could recite portions of *The Canterbury Tales* in Middle English. A painting by his mother hung in his dorm room. He cared about current events. He studied computer programming.

"Programming has similarities to poetry," he said. "The more condensed the language, the better."

He never pressed me to sleep with him.

"We can take it slow," he said.

•

Winter break. I was at a party with friends from high school. I remembered what my mom had said about my dad's grief for Jeanne: "He drank to forget."

I drank to forget.

Two friends carried me downstairs to a bed. They tucked me in, then returned to the party; one of the two stayed behind.

"I've liked you for so long now," he said.

I felt my jeans coming off, my underwear coming off.

"It's just a dream," he said as I tensed up. "It's okay. Everything is going to be okay."

I felt his hand between my legs.

"I've liked you for so long now," he said again.

I moved my mind elsewhere, and when I thought he was elsewhere I opened my eyes.

He was standing with his pants and boxers around his ankles, looking down at me. He was no longer touching me, but I knew what he was doing.

"It's just a dream," he repeated.

I lay rigid, holding in tears.

I closed my eyes and waited until I heard him finish and stumble away.

I remembered my dad saying, "If only I were well enough," as he clenched his cane.

MENTAL ILLNESS

I forgave my friend. I returned to college. I studied. Every night I called my mom. I avoided parties. I performed well on exams. I held on to my scholarships.

I heard voices.

I didn't tell my new boyfriend. I wanted to hold on to him, too.

I was in the middle of a history exam about the development of the modern American city when I heard my name repeated by angry voices.

I stood, sat, stood.

I was inside a big ringing bell.

The other students were in a classroom, answering exam questions.

I walked outside into the cold. The teaching assistant followed.

"What's going on?" she asked.

I paced, sat on the grass, stood, paced some more.

"Fail me," I said.

"Let's go see the professor," she said gently.

She walked me to his office, the same path I walked when searching for my mom and Sharon, and he offered me a seat.

"I studied," I assured him as his assistant left the room. "I'm sorry."

For the next hour my professor asked me about myself. I said I was from Ohio. He too was from Ohio. I said I was studying journalism, but that I also wanted to study poetry and fiction.

"Which writers do you like?" he asked.

I mentioned Henry James. I said that James captures in his letters and books the development of the modern American city.

I described passages I had read from James's notebooks about his travels. In *The Bostonians*, for example, James mentions Delmonico's—one of the first restaurants in New York City.

I remember standing and sitting and standing throughout our conversation. The office felt too small.

"How about you write a paper for me," he said, "and forget the exam. What do you say?"

I thanked him, rushed to the library, and read what I could of James's letters until a sentence about his dead father stopped me: "But he is already a memory, & every hour makes him more so—he is tremendously & unspeakably absent."

•

The next day, a woman from the campus health center called. Would I please come in for a mental health evaluation?

"I'm fine," I told her.

"Someone's very concerned about you," she said. "It's important you come in."

At the health center, I filled out a questionnaire about my mood. Had I ever considered suicide, been sexually abused, cut myself, et cetera? Then I met with a psychiatrist.

"Do you mind if I record our interview?" he asked.

The tape recorder sat between us, his finger poised on the red "record" button.

"I guess not," I said.

He pressed the button, and we began.

"I see you left the question about sexual abuse blank," he said. "Have you been sexually abused?"

I didn't know how to answer.

"By your father?" he asked.

"God no."

"Have you ever considered suicide?"

"My father died. What do you expect?"

Every question he asked seemed to me irrelevant.

"All you need to know is my father died."

He turned off the recorder, prescribed an antidepressant, and a month later I came back full of energy—uncomfortable, restless energy.

"I feel on edge," I told him. "I go running in the middle of the night. And I hate running."

"That's not the antidepressant doing that," he said.

He told me to keep taking the pills, so I did.

•

I sat in the empty campus chapel for daylong stretches and cried.

I wandered along the lakefront between afternoon classes and cried.

I pressed my phone against my ear, pretended my dad was listening, and cried.

I researched how to overdose, slit arteries.

"How are you feeling?" my psychiatrist asked.

I cried.

"What's been happening?" he asked.

"This," I said.

He increased my medication and recommended I attend the grief group on campus.

"You'll meet other students going through the same thing," he said.

MOM

My mom and I spoke every day, but one Friday evening I called and she didn't answer.

Maybe she's still at work, I thought.

I called again.

Maybe she's in the basement, I reasoned, *or maybe her ringer is off.* I let an hour pass.

I called again.

I let the evening pass.

Still no answer.

I called her friend Sharon.

"Your mom didn't have work today," Sharon said. "Is everything all right?"

"I can't reach her," I said.

Sharon volunteered to go to the house. Half an hour later she called me. All the lights were off. Sharon had knocked on the front and back doors several times. Still no answer.

"She probably went to sleep early," Sharon said.

That night I slept with my phone beside me.

The next morning I had a message from Sharon. She'd gone back to the house and knocked several times, yelled my mom's name. Still no answer.

I tried my mom again.

"Hi, Mom," I told her voice mail. "Call when you have a chance. I love you."

Then I called her local police, told them that it was unusual for her not to answer the phone.

"We talk every day," I said.

"When did you call?"

I searched through my call history and reported the precise times.

"A day hasn't passed," the officer said. "Do you think that maybe her phone is off?"

I explained that my dad had died more than a year ago.

"She still wears black," I said. "Can you please go to the house?"

Less than an hour later my phone rang. I looked at its screen: a call from "Mom and Dad."

"My hearing is so bad," she said. "I didn't hear the phone."

I covered the receiver, not wanting her to hear me cry.

MENTAL ILLNESS

"You can't keep crying like this," my psychiatrist said.

He handed me a blue sheet of paper with information about the campus grief group.

"You gave me one already," I said. "I'm not good in groups. I get anxious."

"You need it."

The paper sat crumpled on my desk for weeks before I threw it away.

One evening, on my way to my boyfriend's dorm, I noticed a crisp blue sheet of paper pinned next to a poster about some sorority fundraiser. The group would begin in an hour. I called my boyfriend, asked what he thought.

"Give it a chance," he said.

It met in a poorly lit room on the third floor of a building near the campus chapel. I listened as students shared stories about those they'd lost: a dog, grandparents, a best friend.

"You've been quiet," the leader said, her eyes meeting mine.

"My father died," I said, "and I wasn't with him."

MOM

Then our dog, Gigi, died in her sleep. My mom was left with no one at home. She called to tell me the news.

"Gigi is with your dad now," she said.

I wanted to believe her, but I didn't agree or disagree. Instead, I said I'd visit.

Spring break I took the train to Ohio, and my first day back we visited the animal shelter. A scrawny Brittany was cowering in a cage too small for her.

"She's the one," I told my mom, and my mom agreed. "What do you want to name her?"

"Shu Shu."

"Huh?" I said.

"I like the sound of it."

JEANNE

When I told stories about my dad to anyone, I almost always mentioned Jeanne's death.

I'd explain the circumstances: he gave her permission to go out that night; he didn't know her mother already had said no.

"It wasn't his fault," I'd say, "but he blamed himself."

I understood that her death changed his character, affected the father he was to me. I wondered how he mourned her, and if I was mourning the right way. I talked to him every day, cried every day. I needed to mourn him on Jeanne's behalf, was that it?

I don't know.

I loved him. Wasn't that reason enough?

DAD

Alone in the campus chapel, I prayed to my dad. I told him about my days. I told him I wanted to be with him.

I told him I could see only two reasons to stay alive: my mom, and the book I had promised him.

I wanted him to say, *Your mom will be fine.*

I wanted him to say, *Forget the book.*

I wanted him to say that he was somewhere I could be.

MENTAL ILLNESS

I studied, or tried to study. I never could tell which facts were the facts that mattered. I highlighted almost every sentence in my textbooks, seeing relevance everywhere. And instead of making mnemonic devices, I found ways to connect the material with my dad. The same year my dad was born, James Joyce published *Ulysses* in Paris. One hundred forty-five years earlier, in the same town where my dad was born, the Continental Army hatched plans for the American Revolution.

But if I couldn't connect the material with him, I couldn't remember the material.

The class that I struggled most with was Law in the Political Arena. The professor struck me as smug. When I described him to the maintenance man, I pushed my nose in the air.

One afternoon I asked my professor if I could speak with him privately before class. I asked for his advice—a legal question for my mom: "Her house is across the street from a baseball park and the net doesn't catch the foul balls. So they keep coming into her yard. One of them hit her when she was mowing the lawn." I explained that she lived alone. I explained that my dad had died the previous year. "When I was in high school, he was in his late seventies. So he couldn't take care of the problem."

"I really don't know," the professor replied, and then announced to the class, "Let's get started."

I went to my seat, opened my notebook, and began to take notes. Instead of analyzing what to write, I tried to transcribe everything.

"So let's say we have a man living in a gated community for seniors," the professor said. "He's sixty-five. And he decides to marry a woman twenty-five years younger." The professor laughed. The students laughed. "You know the type."

I raised my hand. The professor looked at me, looked away, and continued.

"The board approves the woman to live there. But now let's say they have a mistake."

This time I didn't raise my hand. I suspected what he meant. I stood.

"A mistake?" I said.

"A beautiful bouncing baby," he clarified. "So now this couple has to move."

"Go to hell," I said.

The walls disappeared. The students disappeared. The professor stood behind his lectern, said nothing.

You should die, I heard. *Get into the ground, Jeannie.*

The voice came from below. I looked at the floor. I was standing on grass.

I gathered my things and walked straight to the campus health center.

"Something is wrong with the medicine," I told my psychiatrist.

"You have to want to get better," he said.

His voice sounded strange. I didn't know how to explain to him that his voice sounded strange.

"Let's try a higher dose," he said.

ELEVEN

This is "The Glass Eye Poem" all over again. When I was in college, that poem swallowed entire days whole.

Writing the poem replaced sleeping.
Writing the poem replaced eating.
Writing the poem replaced talking.
Writing the poem replaced studying.

I finished the poem—according to my professor—one month before deadline, but with the poem done I felt restless, irritable, sad. So I worked and reworked its lines. The last two: "with the help of a black crayon, I / undraw him."

My old drafts are here, next to my desk. My professor insisted I save them. Some of them include my ideas penciled in the margins: "Somehow express the ages of the daughter and father without stating them directly. Maybe have the girl draw her father's face. She'll crumple the paper and hand it to him and say that the wrinkles in the paper are for the wrinkles in his face." I also kept some of my classmates' feedback. Some of them interpreted the ending—in which the daughter blacks out a drawing of the father's face—as showing anger toward the father. I didn't see it that way. The crinkled drawing never existed. It was a detail to demonstrate their ages—as quickly and effectively as possible.

In the poem, the daughter is angry that her father died but not angry at him for dying.

I'm angry at myself for leaving my dad when I did.

If the ending shows anger, it's the daughter's anger at herself—for having portrayed him the way she did in her drawing. The art emphasized his age. It failed to capture the father he was. She thinks the picture must have tormented him, reminding him of how little time they had together.

I received an A and some writing awards for the poem, but it didn't accomplish what I'd meant to accomplish. To me, I'd failed.

This can't be "The Glass Eye Poem" all over again.

MOM

My mom mailed me letters, even though we spoke every day. Usually they mentioned how much money was put aside for me: "I don't want it. At least you'll have something." Always they mentioned my dad: "He often said he wished we had met when we were both younger. We would have had six kids." Even when they didn't mention him outright, he was there: "Sorry about crying on the phone Sunday night. Sometimes I get overwhelmed." Every letter contained: "I love you so much," "I'm always worried about you," and "I'm very proud of you."

The winter of my sophomore year, a letter confirmed that I'd succeeded in hiding from her the extent of my unhappiness. "I'm getting the biggest kick out of you," she wrote. "You're having fun and that makes me happy."

"You always sounded upbeat on the phone," my mom would later tell me. "You would talk about the lectures and poetry readings and how great your professors were. You really did seem happy."

JEANNE

Late one night my junior year, unable to sleep, I opened my web browser and typed "Jeanne Vanasco."

133

If I could understand who she was, then maybe, I thought, I could better understand him.

It never occurred to me to understand myself.

"Did you mean Jeannie Vanasco?" the page of search results asked.

I scrolled past news stories about my being "volunteer of the month" in my hometown, about starting the high school newspaper, about making my college's honor roll. There was my dad's obituary, the one that I should have written. Then there was another obituary. I didn't know he had two.

I opened it.

A New York paper published this other summary of his life. The details were spare, much like in the Ohio version, except that in the list of surviving family members I couldn't find myself. I read it again.

I called my boyfriend.

"I'm listed as Barbara," I told him.

"What?"

He sounded half-asleep.

I tried to explain the obituary.

"Slow down," he said.

"I'd understand if it was my half sisters who did this," I said. "They have their reasons."

"But they know you don't go by Barbara."

I didn't feel like Barbara. I didn't feel like I survived.

"It is accurate," I said.

•

I knew Jeanne was born and raised in Newburgh, New York. I knew she received a medal from a church. I knew she was sixteen when she died in the car accident.

The town, the medal, the accident—those details, however vague, could have led to others.

I could have added "Newburgh" to my search.
   I could have added "car accident" or "medal."
   I could have added her sisters' names.
   Our dad's name.
   My name only confused the search.

I carried my attention elsewhere.

DAD

I planned to live with a friend my senior year, but the apartments she wanted featured gyms, indoor pools, security systems, modern appliances.

"I really want us to be roommates," she said.

The next day she signed a lease with someone else.

My other friends already had signed their leases. My boyfriend had signed a lease. So a friend put me in touch with her friend Rachel who was looking for a roommate.

"I just told someone I'd live with her," Rachel said after we met. "But how about the three of us live together?"

Rachel introduced me to her friend Elizabeth, and a week later they found a three-bedroom on a tree-lined block. The apartment was bigger than my childhood home. I asked about the rent.

"I found cheaper places," I said.

"But this one is such a good apartment," Rachel said. "I'll pay the most."

Her father did something with investments. Her family owned a private jet. They vacationed in places I'd never heard of.

"My situation is absurd," she said. "I could live by myself if I wanted, but I want roommates. Elizabeth's dad is a judge. We should pay more."

"I'll take the smallest room," I told her.

The first few months I'd hear Rachel laughing on the phone with her father or Elizabeth telling hers about her plans to be a dramaturge.

"Dad?" I'd repeat alone in my room, half expecting an answer.

MENTAL ILLNESS

"What are you doing?" Rachel asked.

I was standing over our bathroom sink, running cold water in the dark. My thoughts sounded like radio static.

"Something is wrong," she said, or maybe I said it.

She led me into the living room.

"I haven't been sleeping," I said. "I should sleep."

The windows looked smaller than usual.

•

"I can't help you," my boyfriend said.

We were studying in his apartment for our senior finals. I was on his floor, surrounded by open books. He was on his bed. His mother's painting of a stark landscape, an even proportion of sky and land, hung above him. He might as well have been inside it, he felt so far away.

"I don't understand," I said.

We'd planned to live together the summer after graduation. I'd move to New York in the fall, for an internship at the *Paris Review*, and my boyfriend would maybe follow. "It'll work out," he'd promised.

But now he was citing scenes that I'd tried to forget: he'd stopped me from stepping off a train platform, from throwing myself out of his moving car. I cried too much, he said. I cut.

"I just don't love you anymore," he said.

•

"This is not about your father. It's about your breakup," my new psychiatrist said.

"Wouldn't it be easier for everyone," I said, "if I went back to the old psychiatrist?"

It was too hard to start over, to explain everything again.

But because I'd used my ten allotted free sessions, my previous psychiatrist had referred me to this new psychiatrist, allowing me ten more free sessions.

"Are you sleeping?" she asked, ignoring my question.

"Not really," I said. "Could it be the medicine?"

"It's not the medicine."

•

Twenty-two, there should be twenty-two pills, I reasoned. I was twenty-two years old.

I swallowed the first pile. I'd accomplished something. I swallowed the second pile. I called the campus hotline.

"Something is wrong with me."

I was asked what was wrong with me and I said my thoughts were moving too fast and I took too many pills, "in that order," I specified. The voice asked me to hold. I looked into the mirror and my eye sockets were empty and black. I curled up on the floor and started sobbing into the receiver.

"Hello? What seems to be the problem?"

The campus psychiatrist. That afternoon I'd told her my medication made my thoughts move too fast, and she'd replied, "That's impossible."

"I'm prying open my eyelids," I said, "and there's nothing there."

"Is this Jeannie?"

I swallowed the third pile.

"I don't know. I don't know. I don't know anymore."

•

I remember the ambulance outside my apartment and the streetlamps shaped like question marks. The street sign said Noyes Street, pronounced *noise*.

I felt dizzy. I felt tired. I tried to lie on the grass, but two men pulled me back.

"How many fingers am I holding up?"

"Can you tell us your name?"

Noyes, spelled *No-yes*, how I answered every question. I had lived on No-yes for a year.

•

I opened my eyes. White curtains everywhere. People in white everywhere. A whiteboard on a white wall. "Barbara Vanasco" in thick black marker. A pale nurse with straight black hair and a clipboard. I was in a hospital gown, in a hospital bed.

"Where's my father?" I asked her.

"He's not here," she said, "but we can have someone call him."

I pulled off my sheets. I tried to stand. The emergency room blurred. And my dad, who was somehow still dead, did what he sometimes did—died again, seconds after my waking.

"You need to rest," she insisted, tucking me back in. "Between one and ten, how would you rate your pain?"

"Physical pain?" I asked.

"Any pain."

"Your father never complained," my mom once told me. "He hid his pain. That's the type of person he was."

Ten.

"Three."

"Now what's your father's number?"

I turned over on my side and faced an empty chair.

"I'd like to sleep now," I said.

•

Each time I woke, I felt convinced another day had passed. Fifteen-, twenty-minute stretches of useless dreams, cast without my dad.

"How are we feeling, Barbara?" a man asked.

He dragged the bedside chair closer to me and sat. He was a young doctor.

"Or is it Jeannie?" he asked. "I see two different names on your record."

I wanted to tell the doctor about my first day of kindergarten, when I learned my given name was Barbara Jean, not Jeannie as I had thought.

"Barbara Vanasco," my teacher had said.

No one had answered.

"Barbara Jean Vanasco."

I'd looked around for a girl who looked like me—my parents were the only Vanascos I knew.

"Raise your hand if your name has not been called."

"Do you have a preference?" the doctor asked.

For the first time, I wanted to be Barbara. I almost asked to be called Barbara. Barbara made me feel less like I was there, but Barbara was also my mom's name. Barbara was the reason I'd called the campus hotline; I was staying alive for her.

"I go by Jeannie," I said, "but if Barbara is easier, on account of my records—"

"If you go by Jeannie," he said, "we'll call you Jeannie. Now why did you take so many pills?"

"I thought they would slow things down. They were prescribed."

"How many? For one dose?"

"I miss my father," I explained. "It's normal to go nuts after someone you love dies."

"It's not normal to overdose. It's not normal to hallucinate your eyes have fallen out. It's not normal."

"You lose somebody perfect, then. Then you come back and tell me what's normal."

•

I was taken to a small cramped room on another floor, where a nurse told me to undress.

"Completely?"

"Yes," the nurse said.

I stood there naked while she patted me down. I told the nurse I'd been tricked into admitting myself. Had I not signed the form, she explained, two doctors would have admitted me against my will.

"Do I look mentally ill to you?" I asked her. "Because I'm not mentally ill."

"That's something to talk to your doctors about."

TWELVE

I did talk to my doctors, or thought I did. But my medical records from that first hospitalization allege otherwise.

"She said that she does not feel comfortable talking about her feelings and prefers not to do so," one doctor wrote.

I tried to make the doctors understand: the *i* in my name mattered to me because my dad thought it mattered, because it separated Jeanne from me through language, because language mattered—because how else was I to show my love for my dad, except through language? After he died I wrote him a letter:

> *Dear Father,*
>
> *I never referred to you as my* father *until I lost you. The word sounds distant, conceptual.*
>
> *One letter could make you* farther.
>
> *I miss* Dad.

•

This morning I combed through the latest draft of *My Father's Glass Eye* and replaced most instances of "father" with "dad." "Father" felt forced, too formal, in my mouth. It felt removed, so I removed it.

According to that logic, I could delete his death.

MENTAL ILLNESS

Of course I hallucinated my eyes had fallen out. My dad lost his left eye to a rare disease when I was a child.

And of course that first major breakdown came one month shy of college graduation. My dad died one month after I started college.

But patting my bedroom floor, feeling for my eyes, I couldn't see the significance of my hallucination.

I couldn't see my eyes.

"So you could see everything else," a doctor asked me, "just not your eyes?"

"My dad had a glass eye," I said.

The doctor, despite clipboard and pen, wrote nothing.

I tried again.

"So the hallucination makes sense," I said, and he started scribbling.

I told the doctor that my dad had died. Then I told another doctor. And another.

I told the doctors that my dad had lost his left eye to a rare disease.

"He had a glass eye," I said.

145

It seemed relevant, a metaphor that explained my grief for my dad: How did he see me? Could he see me?

I told them that he'd lost a daughter named Jeanne. I tried to explain that her death at sixteen almost destroyed him, and that his death was destroying me.

"He added the letter *i* to my name," I explained.

I repeated "eye, *i*, I" to them. I had solved the equation that was my identity: eye + *i* = I.

"Do you see now?" I said. "It's all related."

But nowhere do my medical records mention his eye. Nowhere does Jeanne's name appear.

Instead, the doctors focused on my eyes:

"Attractive, slim woman with long eyelashes carrying three books including the latest Paris Review. Cooperative, yet avoids direct eye contact."

"Pleasant but looks frightened. Her affect is blunted and eye contact is poor. Social worker just shared that the patient feels strongly she does not want her mother to know she is here."

"She looked down most of the time during the discussion today and seemed less open in the one-to-one meeting today than in the meeting where there were four of us yesterday."

I tried to talk about my feelings.

"This is grief," I said.

The doctors said grief operated differently.

"Had you known him," I said.

But instead of asking about my life with my dad, they asked how he died.

"I don't know," I said. "He was eighty. He had a lot of things wrong with him."

Natural causes? they asked.

The coroner wrote "throat cancer," I said.

When did he die, they wanted to know.

I told them again and again that he'd died the fall of my freshman year.

"I was eighteen," I said. "Why do you keep asking *when*?"

•

My memory tells me I was hospitalized a few weeks. My medical records tell me a few days. I slept mostly. I have no cinematic scenes. A friend brought me a stack of old *Paris Review*s. Another patient grabbed mashed potatoes off my plate with her bare hands. My roommate, a middle-aged philosophy professor, never said a word (electroconvulsive therapy). At the medication window, a nurse spoke to me in French, and I thought I was losing my mind again— the *Paris Review*s caused her confusion, she later told me. I wrote, and rewrote, the same lines of poetry: "Massaging his iris, a dab of brown, in a soapy film, / cleaning my father's eye in my palm / while he lies between the silver rails of his bed: / this is what the end looks like." And then, in the margins: "But I never touched my father's eye."

What I remember most clearly is sketching my dad on scrap paper: the outline of his broad face, his wide nose, his large brown eyes. I made quick marks on the sides of his otherwise bald head, indicating hair. I used a plain pencil, and so the olive stain of his skin was invisible, the deep brown of his irises invisible, the white of his hair, whiter than the white sheets of paper—invisible.

"What was it about your father?" the doctors and nurses on the ward asked.

What they really meant was, *You're not normal for behaving this way.* And maybe I wasn't.

Maybe I mistook the emotions I felt for unconditional love when in fact they were part of some illness.

Maybe my dad's death triggered something already inside me, some bad gene, or maybe the something already inside me that it triggered was even greater love for my dad.

"What was it about your father?" they always asked, and I always replied the same way: "He loved me."

JEANNE

I left my dad the night before he died. Would Jeanne have done such a thing?

"I wasn't with him," I reminded my doctors again and again.

But they were more concerned with my writing, or about how I was writing: "She reports a decrease in appetite and inability to sleep 'five nights out of seven,' during which she stays up to write."

Elsewhere in my records: "She also states that she 'needs to write.' She further went on to say that she does not have a desire or drive to write but states that she 'shouldn't have to want to write, I just need to write.'"

What did I mean that I lacked a desire or drive to write?

"I'm fine," I said, according to the records. "I just want to go home. I need to be writing."

The records also say: "Obsession, Phobias: has been working/obsessing on one poem the whole school year."

The poem was about him. The obsession was him. Why didn't the doctors direct their attention to my love for him?

They decided I had bipolar disorder. They cited mania. One sign of mania: "pressure of speech." Another: "flight of ideas." Another: "clang associations," connections between words dictated by sound rather than meaning.

To me, "eye" and "*i*" and "I" are connected by meaning. Maybe I was experiencing mania.

I know I was experiencing grief.

MOM

My mom visited the week of graduation. She didn't know I'd been in the hospital, and I made my roommates promise not to tell her.

"You've lost so much weight," my mom said. "Are you eating?"

"I was busy studying for finals," I lied.

Later, she asked Rachel and Elizabeth how I was.

"I didn't know what to say," Rachel told me.

"What did you say?"

"That you're fine."

"You hid that hospitalization from me for years," my mom says. "Why didn't you think you could tell me?"

"You were upset about Dad," I remind her.

"But you could've told me," she says. "I wish you'd told me."

MENTAL ILLNESS

The summer after college graduation, to save money for my move to New York, I worked three jobs, sold some of my belongings (bookcases, an old computer, bed frame, TV set), went to a free public health clinic for my mood stabilizers, and ate mostly oatmeal. After one month of this, my perfectionism snapped.

I drank until I blacked out. I fooled around with men I barely knew. At a party for a Chicago literary magazine, I drank a bottle of wine in the coat closet. Then I left with a writer and we smoked pot from what looked like a cigarette.

"Don't worry," he said, as we circled the block. "The cops can't tell."

I pulled him into a stranger's backyard and we made out on a picnic table. He lifted up my dress and I stopped him.

"This isn't me," I said.

He followed me back to the sidewalk and I started throwing up under a stop sign. Then I remember sirens and flashing lights and two men telling me to come with them to the hospital. I yelled that if I were a man I'd be allowed to puke under a stop sign.

"Someone called 911 for you," one of them said.

The writer and I looked across the street. A cluster of people were standing outside a restaurant, watching.

"I don't have insurance," I told the EMTs.

"She's fine," the writer said.

The EMTs threatened to call the cops.

I started crying. The weekend my dad died, I'd taken an ambulance. I associated ambulances with letting him down.

"Maybe you should go with them," the writer said.

I wanted to hear my dad tell me what to do.

The EMTs helped me into the ambulance.

"What's your Social Security number?" one of them asked.

"Does this mean my mom will find out?"

"No," he said and smiled. "Just say a Social Security number."

So I made up a number. I thanked him.

At the hospital, the nurses and doctors asked the typical questions: Allergies, illnesses?

Afraid of being hospitalized again, I didn't share my diagnosis. "None," I said.

DAD

By August, I'd saved enough money to cover four months in New York. My internship, full-time and unpaid, was supposed to last through December. I figured I'd live cheaply and pick up odd jobs as needed. Before I left Chicago, I found a Brooklyn sublet through Craigslist. The man I'd be living with was going through a divorce, a detail that my mom didn't know.

I packed some clothes and books and family photographs in a green tweed suitcase, the same suitcase my dad carried when he left New York for good, and I moved there.

I'd write a book for him in New York because New York was where his life started.

And I'd never been to New York. I was from the Midwest. I graduated from college in the Midwest. I was used to the Midwest. Why not try somewhere new, where no one knew me?

"You're not from here, are you?" a woman asked the first time I rode the New York subway.

"How can you tell?"

"You're chatting with strangers on the train."

•

I rode the trains and buses, but once, just once, I told myself, I needed to ride in a yellow cab.

I'd otherwise been frugal. For free food, I went to book parties. For free coffee, I went to bank lobbies. For free furniture, I went to rich neighborhoods on trash day. I deserved a short ride in a yellow cab.

I remember when I hailed my first one. I was on the corner of Second Avenue and Tenth Street, standing in the rain with a broken bodega umbrella at my side.

"Where you going?" the cabbie asked.

"Can you loop around the block?" I asked. "Bring me back right here."

"I don't follow."

"My dad, he drove a cab in New York City. Back in the forties or maybe the fifties. I just want to ride in one, at least once."

He nodded and began driving.

"It was more dangerous back then," he said. "That was before they had this glass."

I'd never considered that, the lack of the glass partition. I reached in my bag for my journal. "The lack of glass," I wrote, thinking of my dad's eye, how it wasn't even made of glass.

"So I take it you ain't from here," the cabbie said.

"Ohio originally."

"Miss it?"

"My mom lives there. I miss her."

"Well here we are," he said, stopping where we began.

"How much?"

"Tell me, you ever get angry at your dad?"

"Frustrated sometimes. He was strict, very protective, but I liked that about him. He cared."

The cabbie was quiet and I was quiet.

Rain had never sounded so loud.

He adjusted his rearview mirror. I shifted in my seat. Maybe I read too deeply into his silence, but I sensed he had a daughter he felt distant from, or a daughter who felt distant from him, or who was dead.

"Keep your money," he said. "You're a nice girl."

He drove off with his "Off Duty" light on.

MOM

"I know that Dad didn't want me in New York," I tell my mom. "Jeanne died here—"

"That's not why he didn't want you in New York. He was worried about you being around his family."

"His other daughters? Did he think they'd say things against him?"

"Their mother said a lot of hurtful things to them about your dad. Your dad never defended himself. This is what your aunt Anna and his cousins told me. Anna asked him why he didn't say anything. 'She's their mother,' he said. Your dad's daughters loved him, but they were in a tough position. Of course they're going to listen to their mother. I don't think they know how hard your dad tried. He had a rotten divorce. I wasn't there. So I can't judge."

"She blamed him for Jeanne's death."

"It wasn't just that. From what I understand, the marriage had problems from the start. I'm only going off what your dad told me."

"No one could turn me against Dad."

153

THIRTEEN

My editor calls to discuss chapter twelve.

"The partition in the cab," she says, "was it actually made of glass?"

"The cabbie called it glass," I tell her, "but maybe it wasn't glass—"

"Sort of like your dad's eye."

After we hang up, I research the partitions. Made from a combination of hard and soft glass, the partitions are mostly bulletproof—but not completely impenetrable. That finding seems metaphorical, but I'm trying to move away from metaphor.

I want to focus on concrete details about my dad.

I find a photo of him and me on New Year's. I look to be ten or eleven. We're both in our pajamas. He's holding up a gold bell and smiling. I'm in the front doorway, holding a lidded saucepan. It was something we did on New Year's when I was a child: bang pots and pans on the front porch.

In the photo, he's wearing a white sweatshirt and matching white sweatpants. His clothing choices seem like another opportunity to describe his character.

In the coldest winters, he wore a fake fur hat that looked foreign. The rest of the year, insecure about his balding, he wore newsboy hats or plain khaki baseball hats. He refused to wear anything with a name on it. "Why should I pay money," he said, "to advertise for some company brand?" I repeated this to friends, as if the opinion originated with me. I often claimed his practicality as my own.

In his younger years, he always dressed stylishly. In his brief time at Fort Dix, during World War II, he annoyed his sergeant by not pitching a tent in the rain. Instead, he stood underneath a tent and directed his fellow soldiers. He didn't want his uniform or nice thick hair to get wet.

Traces of those days carried over. In our garage, when he built me toys and shelves, he wore his button-down dress shirts tucked in. But he refused to buy new clothes for himself. For Christmas, my mom put socks in his stocking.

But after I reached high school, he alternated between different pairs of sweatpants and sweatshirts. He no longer could dress himself. I should have known then that he would die. His clothes, though, remained plain; no brand names, no words.

MENTAL ILLNESS

After a few months in New York, I stared at my closet and cried. I stared at my shower and cried. I stared at my food and cried.

While at the *Paris Review*, I'd take breaks that involved crying in stairwells and Tribeca alleys, anywhere I could be less seen. I suppose that's one reason I loved New York City. I could disappear into the crowds. I could cry in public at 2:00 PM or 2:00 AM, and no one noticed.

Rachel, my senior-year roommate, called every morning from her home in Chicago.

"How do you feel?" she asked.

"Like crying," I said.

"You are crying," she said, and we laughed and I cried.

•

With alcohol, my mood lifted. I'd laugh and talk to anyone who'd listen and drink free liquor at parties until bartenders refused to serve me.

Then, at one party in downtown Manhattan, mid-conversation with a writer, his eyes narrowed, squinted, darkened; he hated me. I looked around and everyone in the room wore that same hatred.

"Where are you going?" he said as I walked away and kept walking until I reached my apartment in Brooklyn. I vaguely remember crossing the Williamsburg Bridge.

A doctor said he believed I had schizoaffective disorder and recommended I apply for disability. He worked at a public clinic, which required me to arrive at eight in the morning for an early afternoon appointment. The nurses brought everyone in the waiting room free brown-bag lunches. On the television, a woman always seemed to be throwing a chair and shouting, inspiring the others in the waiting room to begin clapping their hands and shouting.

"What does he know?" I said to Rachel afterward.

"Jeannie, I really think you need to go somewhere for a while—a good hospital. Not these public clinics. My mom said she'll pay for it."

My mom would have done anything, sold everything, to pay for my treatment; I knew this. I remember when she bought herself a brown winter coat at the Salvation Army; that same day, she picked out expensive saddle shoes and a red velvet dress for me. I must have been six or seven. She never called attention to her selflessness; she simply was selfless.

"I'm fine," I told Rachel.

•

After the internship ended, I worked jobs that paid the rent but not health insurance. I pieced together freelance work: manuscript editor for a wealthy French philosopher, research assistant for a documentary TV series about media accountability, administrative assistant to a poet. Jobs that allowed me to avoid consistent in-person interaction. I worked mostly from my apartment or local cafés. I moved from sublet to sublet if I thought my roommates suspected anything was wrong with me. The stress and risk of my unpredictable moods left me afraid to be surrounded by the same people for too long.

MOM

"Maybe you should take a break from writing," my mom says.

Can she tell that I spent an evening crying about my dad's death?

"But I promised Dad a book," I remind her.

"Your dad didn't believe in deathbed promises."

MENTAL ILLNESS

I was crossing Eighth Avenue in downtown Manhattan when I hallucinated my eyes had fallen out. I ran into the nearest drugstore and found a mirror. Was it on the turning stand displaying sunglasses? Was it on the turning stand displaying reading glasses? Either way, there were glasses. I pried open my lids. The mirror angled down, reflecting empty sockets. I blinked and my eyes appeared.

Next thing I knew, I was on a train.

"Socrates feeds you breakfast. Socrates feeds you bacon and eggs. Socrates don't make you leave like the rest of these places," a woman was telling another woman on the train.

I got off. I hailed a cab. I tried making conversation with the driver.

"My dad was a cab driver," I said, "here in New York."

I climbed down to the floor of the cab and held my head.

"You okay?" he asked.

My mouth felt dry. I kept licking my lips.

"Talk to me," he said.

And then I realized: "Socrates is a soup kitchen, isn't it?"

DAD

I called my college ex-boyfriend.

He still lived in an apartment near campus. He worked in Chicago.

"How do I seem?" I asked him.

I didn't tell him about the hallucination.

"How do you feel?" he asked.

"I don't know."

"Let me visit," he said.

So he flew to New York. In bed, he confided that he was with someone else, "but I'll break it off," he promised.

"My dad's first wife cheated on him," I said, "and it destroyed his confidence."

I'd never met the girl my ex-boyfriend was dating.

"Please at least let me help you," he said.

"I don't need anyone's help. I miss my dad is all."

MENTAL ILLNESS

"You can't keep going to these public clinics," Rachel said. "You need a good doctor. So what if it takes a year?"

"A year?" I said.

"My parents will pay."

"No."

"Then you have to tell your mom," Rachel said. "Does she know you don't have insurance? Does she know you need medications?"

I ordered my medications from an online Canadian pharmacy.

"If you don't let anyone help you," she continued, "you're not going to get any better."

The next day, I called Rachel and she didn't answer. I called the day after that, and she didn't answer. I stopped calling and I stopped expecting her to call. I no longer listed her as my emergency contact.

MOM

"It wasn't easy," I tell my mom on the phone, "with you preparing for your death. I'd just lost Dad. And then you were saying things like, 'When I go . . .'"

"I just wanted to make things easy on you for when I die," she says. "Your dad and I always meant well. I know we weren't perfect."

"But you were the perfect parents."

"You can't idealize us. It's not good," she says. "I probably shouldn't have talked about dying, but it's going to happen eventually. I don't want you bothering with all that stuff. I know it's not easy to hear. And I was so depressed. You got to understand, you left for college and then he died, and I was alone with Gigi. And then not long after that, she died. I was just so depressed."

MENTAL ILLNESS

One, two, three years passed, and I visited Sandusky only once. I didn't tell my mom why. I didn't think I needed to explain. She hated being where he died—but she couldn't afford to move. She was stuck in that uneven house, with memories of his uneven breathing.

So she visited me in New York, usually on holidays when she could take more time off from work.

"Maybe we could both move to a more affordable city," I told her on one of those visits.

I think she heard the emptiness in my offer.

"Don't do things for me," she said. "I'm glad you're doing the sorts of things I didn't have the guts to do. You love New York. I can see why."

But the house wasn't the only reason I avoided Ohio. I never could predict my episodes of mania or depression, or mania and depression. Each appointment at the public health clinic, I met a diagnosis I didn't want (bipolar disorder I, schizoaffective disorder, borderline personality disorder)—and I didn't want my mom to know. I worried about her worrying about me.

I forget most of my depressive episodes, maybe because each felt the same. My manic episodes, in retrospect, felt great—but in reality I'd lose friendships over petty arguments and lose money because of impulsive choices, such as booking a one-way ticket to Paris, where I argued with border control—to the point of having my passport stamped with a travel deadline—and soon returned home.

But mania wasn't all bad. A few years after my *Paris Review* internship ended, I met one of its board members, impressed her with my "energy." This was a sentence I heard a lot: "You have so much energy," or "Where do you get all your energy?" She introduced me to the editor of *Lapham's Quarterly*, where she also served on the board.

JEANNE

It was a Sunday afternoon. I was in the office of *Lapham's*, where I now worked, editing an essay about the history of dissection. No one else was there. I often worked weekends because I found it impossible to concentrate around my coworkers. Two of them, I felt certain, thought I was incompetent, and the three of us shared a small room. I wanted to prove to them—and myself— that I deserved the job, but I had to reread everything, it seemed. During our weekly editorial meetings, I forgot my arguments, which I practiced the night before. Afterward, I sat in the stair- well, between the sixth and seventh floors, and cried. On my commutes home, I cried.

"Some mornings, I have trouble dressing myself without cry- ing," I told my psychiatrist.

I had health insurance through work, but I couldn't find a therapist who'd accept it. So I relied on the psychiatrist whose of- fice was only a couple blocks away from *Lapham's*. She prescribed two medications to stabilize my mood and one medication for anxiety. She met with me for five minutes every month. Then she hurried me out.

"What I do is a science," she said. "I see so many people with your symptoms."

I thought of all this while trying to edit the essay. I needed to focus.

The essayist wrote that the English physician William Harvey dissected the bodies of his father and sister. At that moment I felt as if a gust of wind had opened a heavy door. I thought of my dad and Jeanne. What did his body look like in the coffin? What did Jeanne ever look like?

I went online and typed "Jeanne Vanasco" in the search box. I clicked on a link to her high school's memorial page and scrolled down. There, for the first time, I could see her face. I tried to enlarge the small grainy photograph, but she only became more difficult to see: dark wavy hair cut above the shoulders, head turned slightly to the left, a pearl necklace. I stared at the photograph as if looking at her for long enough might allow me to enter the mind of the girl whose death had almost destroyed my dad.

Below the photograph, a childhood neighbor and high school classmate had posted that Jeanne had died in a car accident, along with two high school boys.

MOM

I called my mom.

    "I thought Jeanne was in the car with two other girls."

    "That's right," my mom said.

    "And I thought she was the only one who died."

"That's right."

I told her about the boys.

"Why would he lie about this?" she asked, sounding distressed.

I regretted calling her.

"He could have told me anything and I would have loved him."

She began to cry.

"Dad was probably ashamed that Jeanne died in a car with boys. It was the 1960s."

"I guess so."

But she kept crying.

"He went crazy," my mom reminded me. "Your father told me he almost crashed his car on one of them cement blocks."

I stared at Jeanne's photograph. That my dad had contemplated suicide only reinforced my belief that if you lose someone you love, you lose your mind and that's an entirely natural thing to do.

"He was very depressed when I met him," my mom said. "His daughter had been dead for decades, but he was still very depressed. You don't get over a thing like that."

MENTAL ILLNESS

A sleepless week of writing followed. By Friday evening I found myself in a bed much like the one my dad died in. There, hooked up to tubes, I looked up into the concerned face of a coworker I trusted.

The evening returned to me in fragments: the outline of a house made with pills on my bedroom floor; my phone ringing;

two friends—one of them the coworker—helping me through a doorway, or maybe into a car.

I was in an emergency room.

The doctors explained what had happened: I'd overdosed on mood stabilizers, antianxiety pills, and methadone.

"Methadone?" I said.

And then I remembered: the pills from the online Canadian pharmacy. Before I had health insurance, I'd consulted a friend—who later spent a year in rehab—and he recommended a website that sold prescription medications. I ordered pills, thinking they were mood stabilizers. I took them on and off for a year but stopped when my mood seemed worse. I'd stashed the remaining pills in a shoe box under my bed. To throw them away—even if they weren't helpful—seemed wasteful.

I explained my mistake to my doctors.

I explained to them that my dad had died.

"Recently?"

"Seven years ago," I said. To prove that I wasn't a complete idiot, I added, "Odysseus cried for his wife for seven years."

A doctor returned and informed me that I'd be admitted to a psychiatric hospital in Westchester.

"But my father died."

I tried to explain to him, as I'd been trying to explain all along, that my dad had been a tremendous man.

"This is grief," I repeated.

"You have an illness."

"I have work. If I miss work—"

"You will not lose your job."

"It's not that. People will know."

166

My first day at the hospital, a nurse asked me my name.

"Jeannie Vanasco," I said.

"I have a Barbara Vanasco," she said.

•

For two weeks I was Barbara. The day the hospital released me, my doctor said, "You're a risk-taker, Barbara, and I can see you'll always be a risk-taker. You're not going to change."

I nodded, thanked him for his help.

A friend—the coworker who found me passed out—met me at the hospital, and I asked him on the train ride to my neighborhood, "Do you think I'm too much of a risk-taker?"

"You drink a lot," he said. "You overdosed."

Back at my apartment, another friend joined us. We talked. Or mostly I talked.

Slow down, they said.

Are you feeling okay? they said.

You're talking too fast, they said.

"I'm great," I said, beginning to cry and laugh at once.

They insisted I return to the hospital.

I ran outside, hid underneath a tree in a park near my apartment. My cell phone rang. It was my boss.

"You need the hospital," she told me.

My friends took me in a cab to a different hospital. I stayed only overnight. The doctors determined I was fine.

FOURTEEN

My reaction to my dad's death echoes his reaction to Jeanne's death, but my reaction to her death orbits my interpretation of his reaction to her death, and that interpretation in turn influenced my reaction to his death. I think too much to avoid feeling too much. I think that's it, or I feel that's it.

If I suspend any summary or scenes about his death, his character dies without foreshadowing, paralleling my own experience: I never believed he'd die, not even when hospice arrived.

I've written so much about his death and its effects on me, I've lost sight of my dad's character and my mom's.

Grief isolates me from myself, and it isolates me from them; all I see is his death.

I saw his death when I saw my mom during my early years in New York. I think that's why she's largely absent from my New York scenes—not because I literally didn't see her. She visited.

It's just that on her visits she no longer looked like herself. She looked broken in her unbroken black: black shirt, black pants. If she wore a black skirt, she wore black tights. She was of that generation. She showed her tears when she talked about my dad, and she often talked about him. When we were physically apart, I called almost every day but I tried not to talk about him, not with her, because it hurt to hear her cry.

Still some might wonder: *How did your mom not notice your illness? And why did you think you couldn't tell her?* I'd developed a skill for pretending to be okay. She still doesn't know that I cut my wrists and feet in grade school and junior high. She doesn't know about my friend sexually assaulting me. But eventually she'll read this. (There should be a support group for parents of memoirists.) I can't let myself worry too much about anyone reading this, not yet anyway.

Also, as an adult I didn't think I was hiding an illness. I thought I was hiding grief. She had her own crowded sorrow, and I didn't want to burden her with mine. I like how "own crowded sorrow" sounds, but what do I mean by that? Explaining grief seems like explaining a joke; it diffuses the intensity of emotions. In some ways, it's easier to write about my dad's death than it is to write about my mom's pain.

And now I have this whole other problem. I'm about to include Chris in the narrative. He and I started dating a few months after I discovered Jeanne's picture on the Internet. For the next two years I put my research of Jeanne on hold. Of course those two years with Chris are relevant emotionally, but in terms of my memoir's arc—those years seem irrelevant on a craft level. How do you tell someone you love: *You're irrelevant on a craft level*?

There's probably a better way of putting that.

And one last thing, which seems somewhat minor: one year before I found Jeanne's picture, I adopted two cats from a shelter in Manhattan, and I'm not sure where to put them in the narrative. To include them any sooner seemed distracting from the arc. Right now the cats are asleep on my desk. The black cat is Flannery, namesake Flannery O'Connor, on account of her missing a hind leg (think: Hulga from "Good Country People"). The gray cat is Bishop, namesake Elizabeth Bishop.

"I love you too much to write easily of you," I tell them.

Maybe that's how I'll explain things to Chris.

"Did you say something?" he shouts from the other room.

"Just reading stuff aloud."

DAD

I started dating someone seriously, a poet, a few months after my last hospitalization.

We graduated from the same college, but back then we encountered one another just once, briefly, outside a bookstore off campus. I remember him in a green winter coat with a ripped messenger bag. His friend, a writing classmate of mine, had introduced us: "This is Chris. He did the poetry sequence last year. Chris, this is Jeannie. She's in the sequence this year."

We wouldn't meet again for another four years, at a party in New York.

For our first date, Chris and I went to a poetry reading in Manhattan. Afterward we drank too much in a Brooklyn dive bar and went to see a movie about Keats.

"Do you want to come back to my place?" he asked. "We can read Keats on my roof."

"This is by far the nerdiest and best date I've ever been on," I told him.

For the first time in my life, I didn't think: *What would my dad say about this one?* This is how I knew.

MENTAL ILLNESS

On one of those early dates, Chris asked about my writing, and I mentioned an unfinished essay about my dad's loss of his left eye to a rare disease and my loss of him, "in addition to some other stuff." ("Hallucinations" is what I didn't say.) Abruptly, drunkenly, Chris asked if I was bipolar: "It's not a big deal if you are." When asked how he could tell, he said he just could.

"The diagnosis could be wrong," I told him. "I think the problem is grief. I probably shouldn't tell you this, but you're dating someone with serious dad issues."

•

The first couple of years we dated, I continued working at *Lapham's*—but my moods increasingly, unpredictably, interfered. Sometimes I'd stay in the office, with my anxiety, until midnight.

I'd snap at Chris when I felt like he didn't understand. But he tried to understand. His concern was muffled under the onslaught of my static-sounding thoughts.

"Why don't you just quit?" my mom asked me when I told her how stressful the job was.

"Quit? But what will I do for money?"

"You never used the money that your dad and I saved for your college."

"I can't touch that," I told her.

It was too sentimental.

Chris recommended I apply to a graduate writing program in poetry. I applied to one in Manhattan, was accepted and given enough funding, quit my job, and felt increasingly better.

Soon I moved in with Chris, to Greenpoint, a Brooklyn neighborhood where fonts on restaurant signs mattered, where hair salons and cafés doubled as art galleries, and where a majority of my peers blurred into the same mess of glasses, flannel, skinny jeans, and artful and/or ironic tattoo sleeves.

Our apartment was rent-stabilized, so we overlooked its flaws: narrow rooms, almost no natural light, splinters in the floorboards (the previous tenants had ripped off the linoleum, assuming it hid beautiful hardwood), nightly cameos by cockroaches, and a landlord who micromanaged the recycling and trash. I once disposed of a negative pregnancy test in a garbage can three blocks away, at night when no one could see. But this place was better than my last; there, cockroaches dropped through a crumbling bathroom ceiling, a pipe in the kitchen wall burst annually, and the tenants above fought religiously on religious holidays— "I hate you," "I slept with your best friend," "I've been stabbed."

MOM

My mom and I were speaking on the phone about Christmas. If we booked a train ticket early enough, it'd cost a third of what it cost to fly. I offered to visit her in Ohio. She offered to visit me in New York. And then, seemingly out of nowhere, she said: "I don't understand why your father would have lied to me."

The remark surprised me. Two years had passed since I told her that Jeanne had died in a car with boys. I hadn't considered how the detail would affect her.

"He was probably ashamed," I reminded her.

I moved the conversation back to travel plans.

"It's so boring here," she said. "I'll come to you."

After we hung up, I returned to Jeanne's high school memorial page, clicked on the name of Jeanne's childhood neighbor, Bette, and wrote her an e-mail explaining who I was and asking for any information about my half sister.

Bette responded less than twenty minutes later: "I got goose bumps when I saw Jeanne's name in the subject line." We exchanged e-mails and arranged to speak the next morning.

JEANNE

Bette called as planned.

"You're not going to believe this," she said. "The house where Jeanne lived burned down last night."

I wanted to believe it: I wanted to believe that my dad was behind the fire. I wanted to believe in some sort of afterlife, just as I did when I was a child.

"I don't live in Newburgh anymore," Bette continued. "I live in Arizona, but after reading your e-mail I called a friend who's still in Newburgh and I asked her if any of Jeanne's friends still live there. In her research, my friend happened to hear about the fire and sent me the news article. I'll e-mail it to you. No one died."

I thought of it as a sign: *My dad wants me to stay away from his past, but I need to find proof that he never lied, that Jeanne didn't die in a car with boys.*

"Fred Warmers and George Drennen," Bette said. "After dropping the other girl off, they were driving Jeanne home, and that's when they had the accident. The two boys are linked in the yearbook and class website, though she's not linked to that accident. I don't know why."

"My father said Jeanne was in a car with two other girls and that she was the only one who died. That's what he told my mother."

"You can't imagine how sinful everything was," Bette said. "You were going to go to hell and burn forever if you rode in cars with boys. You just didn't do it. Jeanne's older sister, Carol, she was pregnant when just a senior in high school. She was a cheerleader, very popular and pretty. Her boyfriend, he was a quarterback. The big black shame on the family was her getting pregnant. To follow on the heels of that, not that long after, Jeanne was killed. The reputation the family and girls got from that, you can't even imagine. Have you contacted your half sisters?"

"Not yet," I said. "Can you tell me what you remember of Jeanne?"

"Jeanne was sweet, very kind. I could hear her in the backyard a lot, playing with her little sisters and her cats or dogs. I can't remember which they had. She loved animals. She was a mellow person, happy, very pretty, popular. She had lots of promise."

"What did she look like? The photo online was so small."

"She had dark and thick wavy hair, beautiful eyebrows and eyes, an olive complexion. After you contacted me, I looked you up online and found photographs. You look so much like Jeanne it takes your breath away."

MENTAL ILLNESS

I wanted to call Chris, but he was at his office, where he worked as a development director for an arts nonprofit. He wrote grant proposals to fund music programs in public schools. He organized donor events. He planned concerts. He was busy. I knew he was busy.

Selfish, I told myself as I dialed his work number—*you're being selfish.*

"Guess what?" I told him and launched into the story about Bette and her e-mail.

"Are you sure this is a good idea?" he asked.

"Why wouldn't it be? I mean, I understand why you might think researching my dead half sister is a bad idea."

"I'll be home early," he said. "Or wait—do you have class tonight?"

"I don't think I'll go. Everybody there hates me. And I'm writing bad poems anyway."

JEANNE

"Bette said, 'You look so much like Jeanne it takes your breath away,'" I told Chris as soon as he arrived home from work.

I showed him Jeanne's enlarged yearbook photo, scanned and e-mailed to me by Bette—the same photo that I had encountered two years ago. Jeanne's hair looked dark and thick and wavy. Her eyes looked big and dark. Her eyebrows perfectly arched.

"I don't look like Jeanne," I said.

"You're much prettier," he said.

"Don't say that," I told him. "You can't say that. You're saying that because you love me. Wait—" I grabbed her photo from him. "This is her senior photo. She was sixteen when she died. She was sixteen years old and a senior?"

According to her yearbook bio, her involvement included "Punchinello," "Lassies," "Ushers," "Fashion," "H.R. Cashier," and "Grad Sales." I didn't know what all of it meant, but I planned to find out. Seven of her classmates' photos and bios appeared on the same page. Out of all of them, she was the most involved. But she wasn't in anything her freshman year. I wondered if that was the year she skipped.

Below her bio, two lines of white space. Then: "Deceased."

"Now look what else Bette sent." I handed him the article about the house burning. "The house where my dad lived with his first family caught fire yesterday. Except Bette said it burned down. Actually, only the top floor was destroyed. And my dad was living on the top floor when Jeanne died. Now I know where they lived: 488 Liberty Street."

I showed Chris my research about the house. According to a realty website, the house, built in 1910, was 4,158 square feet: eight bedrooms, four bathrooms, a garage. The exterior was made of stucco.

"Did you do all this research today?" he asked.

"I've known about my dad living on the top floor."

"What?"

I reminded him: "When Jeanne died, my dad and his first wife were separated already. She was living on the first floor with their daughters. I think a lawyer friend of his was living on the second floor. So then this fire could mean that my dad wants me to stay away from his past, not necessarily Jeanne's. He wants me to focus less on him and more on Jeanne."

"I think you need to take a break from all this," Chris said.

"I can't."

DAD

I researched what Newburgh was like when Jeanne was a girl. I found her obituary. She died March 2, 1961—twenty-three years and seven days before I was born. What did March 2, 1984, feel like to my dad? He must have thought about it. What did he think about it? I read self-help books directed toward parents grieving the loss of a child. I read essays by parents who lost a child. I wasn't interested in what psychologists call "replacement child syndrome," a condition seen among children born following a sibling's death.

"Why don't you take a break from this," Chris said.

"The ten-year anniversary of his death is approaching," I said. "I have to keep working."

"I think you should take a break."

JEANNE

Bette gave me the name and phone number of my dad's niece Irene. I'd never heard of her before.

"My mother's sister was married to your father's brother," Irene explained.

Irene went to high school with Jeanne.

"Jeanne was a lot of fun. She didn't have any airs about her. Tall, thin, nice head of hair. A little bit of protruding top teeth," Irene said. "Her accident was a nightmare. At that time they had cars that you could sit three people in the front seat. She was sitting in the middle of the front seat between the driver and the other passenger. The driver was trying to pass a car. She tried to get back into her lane but she lost control of her car. Jeanne was thrown from the car. Killed instantly. Fell on a pile of rocks."

"The driver was a girl?" I asked.

"That's right."

"Bette said Jeanne died with two boys."

"I only heard there were the two girls. One of them is still in Newburgh. I don't know about the other one. There was another car accident that year. Two boys died."

"Do you remember how my father reacted?"

"I'll never forget it," she said. "When the hospital called him, he took off his glasses and broke them in half. He was devastated, beyond devastated."

I remembered my dad in his casket, how I'd put his glasses on him.

"It was the worst funeral I've ever been to," she continued. "The girls were unbelievable. They just cried and screamed. Stuck with me for the longest time. I didn't know her sisters very well."

I asked if the divorce was at all related to the car accident.

"I don't believe so. The marriage was not made in heaven. He was young when he married. She was a little older than him. I don't think he got his chance to sow his wild oats. From what I know, he didn't run around. He was just flirty. He was funny. He was nice. I knew her because we would go to Jeanne's house. She was not very friendly to us kids. I don't know where she is now."

"Maybe all this seems strange," I said. "My researching her, I mean."

"I don't blame you," Irene said. "If it was me, I'd want to know about my other sister. His naming you after her was a wonderful thing. I would have done the same thing. If it gave him comfort, why not?"

FIFTEEN

According to an undated journal entry: "I only feel like 'myself' when I'm writing. I can't write. So I'm not myself. I hurt my hand from slamming my fist on the kitchen table because I can't write."

I organize my journals, my research, and some relevant scraps of prose from earlier writing projects by placing them in color-coded binders. Their organizing principles depend on patterns: this connects to this connects to this connects to this.

In the "Dad" binder I organized my notes according to allit-erative logic. So within "Dad" appear subcategories "Vision" and "Voice." "Vision" concerns his loss of his left eye. "Voice" con-cerns his loss of his left vocal cord. Of course then the word "left" became an issue. So within subcategories "Vision" and "Voice" I marked references to "left" with a blue tab (blue was my dad's favorite color). Later I would address, or try to address, the alter-native meaning of the word "left." One note reads, "What will be left of me when I lose her?" ("her" being my mom).

This brings me to category "Mom." My mom has lost hearing in her left ear. So within "Mom" it also made sense to add sub-categories "Vision" and "Voice." (I considered adding "Hearing," but "Hearing" interrupts the alliterative organizing principle. So I included her hearing under "Voice" because I often need to raise my voice when speaking with her on the phone.)

"Your eyesight is still okay, right?" I asked her when organizing my "Mom" binder.

"Yeah, why?" she asked.

"No reason."

Subcategories "Vision" and "Voice" are deeply relevant in "Mental Illness" because of my voices and visions.

Just as my dad's eye looked real, my voices sounded real—sometimes speaking to me, sometimes about me: *You're stupid* and/or *Jeannie's stupid, yes she's stupid.* Journal entries about hallucinating that my eyes had fallen out are placed within subcategory "Vision" under category "Mental Illness."

JEANNE

I thought about the accident as if I were a reporter.

What was the make of the car?

The time of the accident?

Was traffic heavy?

What was the weather like?

Were there onlookers?

Who alerted authorities? How? This was before cell phones.

Did Jeanne die instantly, like Irene said?

Then I thought about what I could never know.

What were her last thoughts?

Her last words?

What did she last hear?

Did she die with her eyes open or closed?

•

"So your father didn't lie?" my mom asked.

"The neighbor got it wrong," I said.

I told her about Irene. I told her about the Associated Press article that I'd found in the *Oneonta Star* that morning: "Crash Fatal to Newburgh Girl on Rt. 17."

"It ran on March 4, 1961," I said. "Jeanne died on March 2."

I was born in March, and she died in March. How did he feel about that? I wanted to ask my mom if he ever mentioned it, but I let the coincidence hang untouched.

After we hung up, I reread the newspaper article about Jeanne's death:

MONTGOMERY, N.Y. (AP)—A 16-year-old girl was injured fatally when an auto carrying three teen-aged girls went off Route 17K and crashed in a field near this Orange County community Thursday night. Jeanne Vanasco, of Newburgh, died Friday in St. Luke's Hospital, Newburgh. Eleanor Flanagan, 17, of Newburgh, who was injured, was reported in good condition at the hospital. The two girls were thrown out of the car. The driver, Ruth Webber, 18, of Plattekill Turnpike near Newburgh, was not injured. State Police said Webber swung out to pass another automobile, saw a car coming from the opposite direction, swung back into the righthand lane and lost control of her own vehicle.

Tucked in the foothills of the Catskill Mountains, Oneonta is a two-hour drive from Newburgh and covers less than five miles. Route 17 never touches it.

"Girl from Unhappy Home Cold Killer at 16" also ran on the front page that day. Betty Joy Ebert, a Chicago runaway, murdered a truck driver in East Greenbush, New York, an hour-and-a-half drive from Oneonta.

Jeanne lost her life. Betty took a life. The editor made a conscious decision to stack the two stories. *God works in mysterious ways.* Was that what readers thought when they opened the *Oneonta Star*?

•

"Let's have a wall of family photos," I told Chris.

Together we framed photographs of our families, and I noticed that I had far more photos of my dad than of my mom. And then I found a photograph of Arlene, my dad, and me from when I was four years old. A white patch is taped over his left eye. He's smiling, standing behind Arlene and me at the kitchen table. Arlene holds me on her lap. Her thick dark wavy hair falls below her shoulders and blends in with mine. We all have the same olive skin. She looks like my sister. She called me her sister. I was never her "half sister."

"Isn't she beautiful?" I said to Chris, handing him the photo. "Carol and Debbie were beautiful. Jeanne was beautiful."

Then my phone rang.

"It's Bette," I told Chris. A few months had passed since I last spoke with her. "Isn't that strange? I was just talking about Jeanne."

Bette said that my dad's first wife had died.

"Have you contacted your half sisters yet?" she asked.

"Not yet," I said. "I will. But I should wait, what with their mother's death. They were very close to her."

MENTAL ILLNESS

"I think you should stop," Chris told me. "This research is clearly upsetting you."

I tried following his advice.

When Bette e-mailed, I delayed replying. When I finally replied, I made excuses for my delays.

But Bette continued reaching out. How could she know about my unpredictable mania—and the depression that snuck into mania?

I doubted I could hold a job after graduating from the poetry program. But I needed some way to pay rent, and my freelance work felt increasingly hard to piece together.

So I applied to another graduate writing program, this one in memoir, at another university in Manhattan. If I tried to write a memoir, then I'd have to continue my research.

I could lean on student loans if I needed. I could find health insurance through the university. Then I could have two more years to figure out the correct combination of medications. I'd read somewhere that it takes between five and seven years, on average, for someone with severe bipolar disorder to find the right combination. I just needed more time.

The program accepted me, and it was funded. Now I had an excuse to continue with my research. Maybe I'd finally finish the book I promised my dad.

DAD

I stepped back from Jeanne. The book, I decided, would be about my dad's life—and I wanted to start writing it before my memoir classes started.

He was born in a wood-frame clapboard house when electric and horse-drawn trolley cars still ran through his hometown, a city on the west bend of the Hudson River.

His first language was Italian.

His birth certificate lists him as Giovanni Battista Vanasco, but the 1925 census lists him as Terry Jr. Vanasco. He was three years old.

I tried to find his army records, but in 1973 they were destroyed in a fire at the National Personnel Records Center in St. Louis.

JEANNE

Bette reached out again, put me in touch with one of Jeanne's high school friends, a woman named Larraine. In an e-mail, Larraine wrote of Jeanne: "She was tall, slim, pretty with long dark hair and dark eyes. She was liked by everyone and had a great smile." I didn't reply.

Bette updated Jeanne's entry on the Newburgh high school's memorial page. It no longer said that Jeanne had died in a car with two boys. I thanked Bette.

Soon spring spilled into summer.

I helped manage a citizen journalism project based in Sudan. I worked remotely from my apartment, editing news reports of genocide.

I taught high school students in the Bronx.

Summer spilled into fall. I threw myself into more research about my dad.

I tried to adopt an eyeless dog.

DAD

I was in my neighborhood, in McCarren Park, writing in my notebook, when Chris showed up. He was wearing the same blue plaid shirt he'd worn the day before. I sniffed him, then he sniffed himself and shrugged, shook his head as if to say, *I don't smell.* I closed my notebook, slipped it into my bag.

"It's pet adoption day," he said and pointed to the other side of the park.

Somehow I hadn't noticed the tents or heard the music.

"I think Flannery and Bishop might like a small dog," I told him.

"I don't know," he said. "I was just thinking we'd look."

As we approached a circle of tents, one of which included a DJ, I mentioned that I was thinking about visiting Newburgh. Before he could tell me it was a bad idea, I said: "What jerk hires a DJ to play at pet adoption day?"

In a tent next to the DJ's tent, a small white dog was pacing underneath a table.

"Why would they play loud music with all these dogs?" I continued. "Look at that poor white one."

I grabbed Chris's hand and pulled him toward the dog.

"Are its eyes sutured shut?" he asked.

I hadn't realized. I ran over, leaving Chris, and learned from a man whose name tag read "Volunteer Joe" that a jogger had found the dog in a park in Queens, her fur matted and her eyes badly infected. She was about seven years old.

"The vet thinks animals attacked her," Volunteer Joe said. "That's why her eyes had to be removed."

I knelt and petted her, she nuzzled my hand, and I asked for an application to adopt. Chris was distracted at some other tent.

"Our cat Flannery lost a leg," I told Volunteer Joe while I hurriedly filled out the application. "Before I adopted her, I mean; I didn't do it. And our other cat, Bishop, had an injured hind paw when I adopted her. So the eyes, or no eyes, are not a big deal."

I was writing on the form why I wanted Milly (her name would be Milly, I decided, after the blind poet John Milton) when I heard Chris say, "There's a Victoria's Secret model here."

I nodded and continued writing.

"Not like I care," Chris said. "It's funny is all. What are you doing?"

"I'm just filling out an application," I said. "I'm not going to adopt her or anything."

"Adopt who?"

"Milly," I said.

"The eyeless dog?"

"Just putting my name in, you know?"

A week later, a woman visited our apartment to interview Chris and me about our relationship.

"What I need to know," she said, "is can you provide a stable home for this dog?"

•

While I planned my trip to Newburgh, Chris researched how we could arrange the apartment to meet Milly's needs. He was pricing playpens online.

"I guess I could bring her to work with me," he said, "on days you can't be with her."

"I'm just worried about Flannery and Bishop," I said. "Will they adjust? I don't think they'd hurt her."

"Maybe they'll empathize," he offered. "We'll be a home for disabled animals."

Flannery scratched at her head with her phantom leg. I shined a laser on the wall and Bishop chased the small circle of light.

"By the way," I began, "I've decided to visit Newburgh."

JEANNE

I entered the graduate program in memoir just as I was finishing the graduate program in poetry. If acquaintances—even some friends—asked why I was doing another writing program, I told them that I was writing a book of creative nonfiction. I changed subjects before the next presumed question: About what? I was still in my twenties. I didn't want to be told that I was too young to write a memoir. I didn't want to be told that there were enough grief memoirs being published. I didn't feel like defending my decision to write about my dad. I also didn't want to mention mental illness.

But to my memoir professor and eleven classmates, I could say I was writing a memoir.

The first day of class, we sat around a large table on the twelfth floor. One of the walls was a window. Outside, skyscrapers and clouds.

"My memoir is called *My Father's Glass Eye*," I said. "It's about my father. I use his loss of his left eye as a metaphor for my grief. He died when I was eighteen. The book is also about his loss of his daughter Jeanne, my half sister. She died in a car accident when she was sixteen. He named me after her, except he added the letter *i* to my name. Mental illness sort of figures into it."

I explained the sonic thesis that held the story together: eye + *i* = I.

Meanwhile, I thought: *What did the skyline look like when my dad lived in New York, he never wanted me in New York, would he like where I live, would he approve of my memoir?*

After class, my professor told me that my memoir was not about my dad or mental illness.

"This is about your experience of having a dead half sister," she said. "The eye stuff, save that for another book."

She recommended I let go of the sonic thesis.

"What if I don't present it as a mathematical equation?" I asked.

"Focus on your half sister," she said.

•

"What would I even write about my dead half sister?" I asked Chris.

He was sitting on the couch, against our wall of family photos in mismatched frames. Joseph Brodsky's *Collected Poems in English* was open on his lap.

"Maybe," Chris said, "you could include—but not focus on—your half sister?"

"I was already planning on that, but my professor wants it to be all about my half sister."

Chris recently had won a major national poetry award, and I felt embarrassed by even attempting to write. If he heard me tell anyone that he was the better writer, he'd say I was wrong. In addition to embarrassment, I felt guilty. His development job at a music nonprofit consumed his life. I had more time to work on a book.

"Those photos on the wall," I said. "I just noticed: I appear either with my mom or with my dad, but none of them show the three of us together. That could be metaphorical."

"That's interesting," he said.

"Or simply logistical," I continued. "There were only the three of us together usually. So who else was going to take the photo?"

Bishop jumped on the couch. Flannery crawled onto my lap.

"I hope we get approved to adopt Milly," I told Chris.

"We will. Now let's go to sleep."

"I might stay up and write," I told him.

"You should sleep. You know what happens when you don't sleep."

•

I called the cemetery's main office and was told where Jeanne was buried: section M, plot 369.

"She's double-deep," the cemetery worker said.

"Double-deep?"

"Her mother is buried on top of her. They share the same plot."

"What about the plot next to it?" I asked. "My father had bought it for himself."

"Your father bought it so it belongs to him."

"If he's dead," I began.

I explained that he'd lost the plot in his divorce, but then his ex-wife offered it back to him. I said that he chose to be buried in Ohio.

"It's listed here as belonging to him," the cemetery worker said. "Did he leave it to anyone in his will?"

"Not specifically," I said. "He wanted everything of his to go to me."

"Then it belongs to you."

"Even if he didn't specify? I doubt he ever thought I'd look into his empty cemetery plot."

"It's yours."

SIXTEEN

For three hours now I've revised the same page.

I hate the sudden shifts of mood that happen throughout the day. How do I articulate but not experience them? Lately it's been hard to write without crying.

Maybe I should move my memories and research into one binder, the "Dad" binder. "Mom," "Jeanne," and "Mental Illness" could fit within it—separated by dividers.

But I don't want to give up the "Mom" binder.

I could keep the binders as they are, and within each binder could be the other binder categories. So within "Mom" would be "Dad," "Jeanne," and "Mental Illness." But then I worry about duplicate passages—because so much overlaps.

What's my hindsight perspective?

Is this my narrative present?

If I could organize my thoughts, I could organize my writing.

I should stop today and start again tomorrow.

DAD

In my pages, my dad didn't seem human, some of my classmates told me. He lacked flaws.

"Don't you resent him for naming you after his dead daughter?"

"What about him being so old when he had you?"

"Do you think it was irresponsible?"

"But he knew he wouldn't survive much past your adolescence. How could he? He was so old."

MENTAL ILLNESS

Chris booked a flight to Indiana to see his parents.

Before a cab picked him up for the airport, we hugged and kissed as if he were leaving for war.

"Let me know as soon as you get there," I told him.

Shortly after his plane landed in Indiana, meteorologists predicted a deadly hurricane on the East Coast. They named it Sandy. Chris called from his parents' house and launched into exhaustive hurricane safety tips. Apparently our street divided two different zones. Our side could experience flooding, but it seemed unlikely. Chris said he had e-mailed me the details, something about the zones being numbers, letters, or colors.

"You'll only be gone for two weeks," I reminded him.

"Had I known—"

"It's good you're visiting your parents. I'll be fine. I'll write and play with the cats."

Of course I couldn't write the entire time, nor—as tempting as it sounded—only play with the cats. So I meandered around the neighborhood, brainstorming my options. My mom had called three times already. I definitely should call her back. But first I needed to make a plan. I could paint the walls. I'd be stuck in the apartment anyway. I was thinking a soft green accent wall for the kitchen—maybe around the two big windows overlooking the landlord's garden. I stopped by the local hardware store for paint, then, on my way home, visited the kitchen store, where cookie cutters of the non-boring, non-holiday variety—dinosaurs, giraffes, dogs—were half off. I was never someone who particularly enjoyed baking, but maybe I'd start. Or I could hang the cookie cutters from nails on the new accent wall. I ended up spending fifty dollars, but really I was buying more than cookie cutters. I was buying décor.

My mom called again and I answered.

"Are you inside?" she asked. "Do you have enough groceries?"

"I'm running errands," I told her. "I'll get groceries and then I'll be home very soon. I love you."

"I love you, too. Call me as soon as you get home. Please."

After we hung up, I walked toward my apartment and thought about Sandy. Couldn't the meteorologists have chosen a more menacing name? Monosyllabic, perhaps? Anything from Norse or Greek mythology would be cliché. But it couldn't be something too contemporary either. I didn't want to know someone whose name also linked to a natural disaster. I wondered if anyone had written about the gendered naming of storms. I wondered if someone named Sandy had broken a meteorologist's heart. I wondered what Chris would have named the hurricane.

I stopped underneath the Brooklyn-Queens Expressway, set down the paint and bags of cookie cutters, and called him.

"What's that noise?" he asked. "Where are you?"

I was under the BQE, in some small, relatively empty parking lot where the only vehicle was a rusted van with no wheels. But I didn't tell him that. Instead, I said: "I'm on our street."

"What's going on there?" he asked. "Are those sirens? You should be inside."

"Aw," I told him, "I can see Flannery in our window. Hi, Flannery."

Then I told him all my ideas for the apartment.

"Please don't paint anywhere near windows during the hurricane," he said. "Stay out of the kitchen as much as you can. Go to the living room, where we don't have windows."

"I'm not stupid," I said, while mentally revising my plan. "All of this is for *after* the hurricane."

"I really am sorry I can't be with you," he said. "I love you."

"I love you too. I'll be fine. I should go. I should get inside the apartment."

But first I went to the local office supply store and bought binders and dividers and notebooks and sticky tabs and pens in various colors. If I experienced trouble writing, I'd organize my writing. I'd color-code scenes involving the different characters.

I'd color-code repeating imagery and symbols. I'd give each character his or her own binder and within the binder I'd organize . . . I wasn't sure yet. I'd figure that out.

Soon I was back under the BQE, this time with two bags of office supplies slung over one shoulder, and the paint and bags of cookie cutters at my feet. I considered hailing a cab. A red car slowed alongside me. The driver rolled down his window, asked, "Are you okay carrying all that?"

"Yep," I said.

"You sure? A storm's coming."

"I'm almost home."

"You live around here?"

"With my boyfriend, yes."

"Why ain't he helping you?"

"He's on duty."

"He's police?"

I nodded yes, and the car shrunk away. I suddenly remembered: I'd forgotten to ask Chris what he would have named the hurricane. I'd call later.

Back at the apartment, I found Flannery and Bishop running around nervously and scratching the couch. The cats proved excellent meteorologists. The storm was about to arrive. So I printed my manuscript—which mostly consisted of scenes from my childhood—and then huddled in the living room with the cats and my new writing supplies.

I began by cutting out individual, representative sentences from my manuscript, such as: "I closed my left eye, then my right, a game of illusions that moved objects, moving my dad an inch each time." I then glued each sentence to its own piece of paper and expanded on the sentences. I was deepening the smaller narratives in order to find the bigger narrative. Meanwhile, the cats were running around, scattering loose sentences around the living room. Flannery had a sentence in her mouth, but before I could tear it out she swallowed it. Now I didn't know what I was missing.

My head ached, and the wind and rain weren't helping. They sounded like someone trying to break in. That guy hadn't followed me home, had he? No, of course not. I closed my eyes and lay on the floor. What time was it? I looked at my phone, and it was dead, and I'd forgotten to call my mom. I should sleep. I'd call her after I slept

But I shouldn't sleep in the front room, our bedroom, because of the windows. Maybe I shouldn't sleep—because of all these ideas for the book. What ideas? Too many to write. It was just a matter of which to write first. What if tomorrow I woke up and couldn't write?

I couldn't sleep. So I returned to cutting and gluing sentences but was losing the inspiration to write more sentences inspired by those sentences. I decided to record audio. I'd record what I wanted to write, and then I could transcribe the recording. Except that wasn't writing, was it?

What was writing, really?

The hurricane was a metaphor. It was a metaphor for grief. Even though it was bearing down on me, I was supposed to write as if I were outside the hurricane, observing the hurricane. I could see the destruction but I wasn't in it. That was how this was supposed to work. Was it ethically problematic that I was using a deadly hurricane as a metaphor for my grief? Was it unethical that I was writing nonfiction about the dead—who could never explain themselves? It was. It was.

Groceries. I'd forgotten to buy groceries.

•

The storm ended, and I was disgusted by my sorry attempts at writing. Our apartment hadn't even flooded. So many other New Yorkers had lost their homes. Maybe I could donate to the Coalition for the Homeless and any hurricane relief funds? Directly helping animals seemed manageable. I contacted an animal rescue nonprofit and arranged to foster cats. When a staffer at the rescue organization brought two kittens to my apartment, she said they'd been abandoned during the storm. So I nicknamed them Sandy cats. She asked if she could call their other cats Sandy cats.

"I don't mind," I said.

Turned out it was successful marketing. A few days later she reported that any cat called a Sandy cat—no matter how old— was fostered or adopted almost immediately.

I wanted to brag to Chris, but I didn't want to tell him quite yet about the kittens. I felt bad not asking him first—even though I felt sure he wouldn't mind. It was Flannery and Bishop I was worried about. Those two knew something was up, and the kittens—it turned out—did not get along. The white kitten terrorized the tuxedo kitten, biting his ears and tail until the tuxedo cried and jumped on my lap. So I had to separate the kittens and, in addition, keep both of them separate from Flannery and Bishop. I was running back and forth between all four, petting each one for equal amounts of time.

Then I learned through the news that some senior citizens were missing from their nursing homes—it had all happened during the hurricane. I contacted a friend from undergrad who worked for a think tank. I explained my plan for a seniors' registry.

"I'm having trouble following," he said.

"I'll think on this some more. I just need to flesh out my ideas for sign-in sites. I'll be in touch."

•

A few days later, I listened to one of the recordings I made during the hurricane:

> *This book should not be that difficult. I'm being too ambitious. I'm making it too difficult. I'm too difficult. I don't mean to be. I need to try harder all around. What I need to describe is my experience of being named after a dead sibling. Except I haven't thought about her as much—as constantly as I do—until now. Except—Except. I say "except" a lot. I wonder why it sounds the same as "accept." Except I accept my name. Except I don't accept his death.*

I sounded idiotic—and yet I couldn't bring myself to delete the recording. Was I a digital hoarder?

I circled around the neighborhood, thinking about lost seniors and homeless animals, homeless people and my home back in Ohio, mania and the depression that usually slid in afterward. I wasn't manic though. In the recording I was talking fast, and sure, the "except"/"accept" part was sort of manic-y, but if I were manic I wouldn't be worried about mania. I didn't think so anyway.

A sign planted outside the local American Legion, just a few blocks from my apartment, read: DROP OFF DONATIONS FOR SANDY VICTIMS HERE. I ran back home and picked out coats and shoes that I knew I wouldn't wear anymore. I carried armfuls of clothes there.

Wouldn't my dad be proud of all I was doing? I was helping animals and helping hurricane victims. I was trying to help lost seniors, and eventually I'd paint an accent wall in the kitchen. My dad had been a maintenance painter. And a senior. And he'd loved animals. I didn't know if he'd ever experienced a hurricane. Although I could research that. And I still needed to inquire about Milly.

Chris called, said he would come back tomorrow.

"Okay," I told him, "there's something you should know."

I told him about the kittens.

"That's fine," he said. "But we're not keeping them, right?"

"No, no, no. I'll find a permanent home for them."

I also explained that I hadn't yet painted or hung the cookie cutters. I also told him that I gave away some clothes. I possibly, accidentally, donated one of his shirts.

"But I'll buy you a new one."

"Are you okay?" he asked. "What's going on?"

SEVENTEEN

I listen to another recording I made during Hurricane Sandy:

> *I repeat myself. I don't know the order in which I'm supposed to explain myself. I made the promise, I think, because I wanted to keep him alive, I wanted another way to spend time with him. I knew he would die. Why else did I make the promise? So why did I leave him?*

If I never finish the book, my dad would understand, and if he wouldn't it doesn't matter. He's dead.

JEANNE

"What's your plot?" my professor asked me in her office. "You don't have a plot."

"What if it's about the promise to write the book?" I asked.

"Writing the book can't be the plot of the book," she said.

"You're probably right. I don't know why—"

"Your book is about your search for your dead half sister."

•

How is it that I know the difference between story and plot, and yet I can't make plot work on the page?

According to E. M. Forster: The king died, and then the queen died—that's a story. The king died, and then the queen died of grief—that's a plot.

The father dies, and then the daughter loses her mind—that's a story.

The father dies, and then the daughter loses her mind from grief—that's a plot.

"Everyone's parents die," my professor said. "This can't be about that."

MENTAL ILLNESS

The animal rescue organization approved my application to adopt Milly, but they wanted $400. I'd expected the fee to be $150, max. Also, Milly was not in their Brooklyn location. She'd been moved to Long Island.

"I'll have to rent a car to pick her up," I told the rescue worker. "Is there any way you can reduce the adoption fee?"

"No."

"Oh. The animal shelters in Manhattan don't charge that much. I understand you have overhead costs, but—"

"Four hundred dollars."

"I'll need to talk it over with my partner."

She hung up without saying good-bye.

•

"The living room is a mess, like my manuscript," I told Chris after he returned from Indiana. "Also, the kittens are still here. Also, Milly is going to cost us $400."

"What? Four hundred? She's seven years old and doesn't have eyes."

I rocked the tuxedo kitten like a baby. The white kitten played with a hair tie in our bed.

"Just because she's older and doesn't have eyes doesn't mean she should be worth less money," I told him.

"You know what I mean," he said. "How many people are really trying to adopt a special-needs dog with sutures for eyes?"

"We could manage the kittens."

He hugged me.

"So that's a yes?" I asked.

•

The woman from the animal rescue picked up the kittens. Turned out she'd found a home for them. So now Chris could pretend like he'd wanted to keep the kittens.

"You know I wouldn't have told you no," he said. "I went along with the eyeless dog."

"Her name is Milly, or would have been Milly."

"I researched playpens for Milly," he said.

JEANNE

A classmate told me that Jeanne is pronounced the same as Jean.

"Some people pronounce it the same as Jeannie," I said.

"I don't think you're right," she said.

Back at my apartment, I searched YouTube for videos of women named Jeanne. I found a TV news story about the soap opera star Jeanne Cooper. And yes, she pronounced her name with two syllables. I considered sending this proof to the classmate.

But I didn't want to seem like I cared that much. Because anyway, I had already decided that my book wasn't about my half sister.

•

I called my mom.

"Dad's daughter who died, her name is pronounced the same as mine, right?"

"That's right," my mom said. "Why?"

"I might include more of her in the book."

DAD

"It's hard for me to read your writing," a classmate told me. "I didn't have a good father. That's why I want to know more about why you loved him so much. I just didn't know it was possible."

JEANNE

"Why do you think you're obsessed with Jeanne?" my therapist asked.

"I'm not obsessed," I told him.

"What would you call it?"

My therapist was young and well-read—many of our meetings began with one of us asking the other, "Have you read this book?" He worked for a counseling center that accepted payment on a sliding scale. I started seeing him shortly before I started the memoir program, and I trusted him. I didn't lie to him, at least I didn't mean to; I really didn't believe my interest in Jeanne was unreasonable.

"I'm curious," I said.

"Why do you think you're curious about Jeanne, then?"

"Maybe I'm trying to convince myself that my father loved me less than I know he did."

"Why?"

"I need to stop missing him so much."

MENTAL ILLNESS

I sat at a picnic table in the park, trying to write after a two-hour walk failed to calm me. I couldn't stop berating myself aloud. So I chose empty side streets and struggled not to speak if anyone was nearby.

If I couldn't control my voice, how could I control my writing?

•

After a workshop, a classmate told me: "Your psychosis scenes are the most interesting. But I'd like to see more scene-setting within those."

"I don't really remember, I guess I could re-create, but then—"

"The mental illness stuff," she said, "is the most interesting. There definitely should be more scenes of you losing it."

JEANNE

Was my classmate wrong about adding scenes of my psychosis? She'd been wrong about the pronunciation of Jeanne's name. I never told her. Should I have told her? No. It would have seemed like it bothered me, and if she thought it bothered me then she'd call Jeanne the internal conflict.

But was I manufacturing conflict in order to construct plot?

•

Bette called again, recommended I contact a writer named Genie.

"Spelled G-E-N-I-E," Bette said, and my hand shook while I wrote down the name. "She may be able to help you."

Genie wrote a novel set in 1950s Newburgh, and her father served as city manager around the time Jeanne died.

So I e-mailed Genie, and she replied within minutes.

"Visit Newburgh," she said. "You can stay with me. I have plenty of room in my house."

We arranged a date. It happened to fall the same month as the ten-year anniversary of my dad's death.

"Given the timing," Chris said, "are you sure you want to go?"

"I'll be fine," I told him.

That night, I lost control of my voice.

"Jeannie's going to die," I said to my bathroom mirror. "Jeanne's dead."

I didn't tell Chris.

MENTAL ILLNESS

Chris and I were walking to a friend's dinner party in our neighborhood.

"Dinner parties shouldn't happen until your late thirties," I said. "I feel like a kid playing dress-up."

My right shoulder shot up, and my head shot down to meet it.

"I don't think I can go," I said.

"What's happening?" he asked.

My neck twitched hard and fast.

"Imagine being blamed for your child's death," I said.

He walked me home. He insisted on staying with me.

"I'll be okay," I said. "I'll be more upset if you don't go to the party."

After he left, I washed my face. When I looked into the mirror, I heard a voice say: *Cut your eyes out. You're supposed to know what it's like.*

JEANNE

Despite Chris's attempts to convince me to stay, I took a train to Beacon, New York. Genie was waiting outside her car when I stepped off the train.

"Jeannie!" she said. "I'm Genie."

Genie was petite and delicate-faced. She hugged me, said she was so happy that I'd be staying with her for the weekend.

"Isn't it funny?" she said. "Same name. Different spellings."

As we drove into Newburgh, we passed rows and rows of once-stately houses: broken and boarded-up windows, peeling paint, crumbling porches.

"Newburgh's changed," she said. "It was a different town when I was a girl. Oh, you'll never believe this, but I mentioned you to my neighbor Verna, and she knew Jeanne. They went to school together. Would you like to meet her? I can tell you about the town, and she can tell you about your stepsister."

"Actually, Jeanne is my half sister," I said.

"Half sister. I forgot."

"It's just, she and I share the same dad." My shoulders tightened. "Half sister, stepsister. It doesn't matter. I'd love to meet Verna. It's so kind of you to be helping me."

"Of course. This is all so interesting."

As Genie drove, she told me about Newburgh—but my thoughts drowned out her voice. She pulled in next to a huge house.

"This is us," she said, and I followed her inside.

She handed me a framed Jewish poem about names.

"My daughter gave this to me years ago, and I think you'll find it interesting, given everything," she said and then left the room to call Verna on the phone.

I sat on the couch, reading the poem to myself—"each man has a name given him by the seasons of the year and given him by his blindness"—when I heard a voice from outside say, "Genie? It's Verna."

"Verna?" Genie said from another room. "I was just about to call you."

Just as Genie came into the room, Verna opened the door, saw me, and stopped. "Oh my gosh," she said, "you look so much like Jeanne. Yes, you look like a Vanasco."

I didn't know how to respond.

"Thank you for doing this," I said. "It means a lot."

We sat at the kitchen table. Genie poured us coffee, and I asked Verna what she remembered of Jeanne.

"Very nice girl. Friendly, warm. Popular. Gorgeous."

I tried pressing for more details. I didn't expect too much. More than fifty years had passed since Jeanne died.

"She always dressed nicely," Verna said. "I remember she had the prettiest camel skirt. Real camel hair. Now that was class. I can't believe I'm remembering this but the day she had that on, she also wore a white blouse and a blazer. We were at Walt's. She and I would often stand in Walt's and talk."

"Walt's?" I said.

"A bunch of us used to go to lunch, especially juniors and seniors, to this place on Bush Avenue. Walt's, it was called. We would all walk down in groups and get sandwiches and sodas and we'd eat there standing. That's where I'd always meet up with Jeanne. And gee, I really, really liked that girl. She was a very nice person. I always felt that way about her. Very well-liked. Very well-liked. If you heard the name Jeanne Vanasco, you would think, 'Oh, she's so nice.' You would never hear a negative thing about Jeanne, ever."

"Did you go to her funeral?" I asked.

I thought of my half sisters screaming at Jeanne's casket.

"I tried to go," Verna said, "but the funeral was mobbed. I couldn't get in. The whole church was packed."

My chest tightened. I thought: *I shouldn't be upset about Jeanne's death. Jeanne wasn't my sister to grieve.*

"Did you hear anything about my father's reaction to Jeanne's death?" I asked.

"I remember knowing that he took it very badly. Now how I knew that, I don't know. But you know how everyone talks to everyone."

"Do you remember my father very well?"

"I remember him with white hair and glasses. Just vaguely. I met him only once. It was after some political dinner. A friend asked me, 'Can you give my friend Terry a ride home?' And I said, 'Of course.' At the time he lived in New Windsor, in a pretty little section across from Calvary Cemetery. I knew he had taken the death badly. That's why I didn't go into too much detail in the car that night. I said I liked Jeanne and what a shame it was. He said, 'Nothing has been the same since.' I only met him that once. Two years had passed since Jeanne died, maybe longer. I remember he seemed very sad."

DAD

"My dad moved to a house across from the cemetery where Jeanne was buried"; I wrote that sentence over and over in my journal the night after I learned of his move.

"There's nothing worse than outliving your child," my mom says on the phone. "I can't even imagine. That's the sort of thing that'll drive you mad."

Did my dad stand in his front yard staring at the cemetery gates, thinking of Jeanne, thinking of his body in the ground next to hers?

But he lost his cemetery plot in his divorce.

Do I regret never having contacted his first wife? No. Do I hate her for blaming my dad for what wasn't his fault? No. What we say and do in grief is inexplicable.

"She also lost a daughter," I tell my mom.

"That's true. When your father died, I didn't know what I was doing."

JEANNE

I stood with Genie outside the house where my dad and his first family had lived.

Building permits were taped to the front windows. The third floor's pale gray exterior clashed with the dirty yellow of the house's lower half.

"It's huge," Genie said.

I photographed the beige picket fence. I photographed the rosebush. I photographed the exposed brick pieces of the mostly paved street. I photographed the windblown leaves scattered along the side yard. The street where we stood sloped down toward the Hudson River. Telephone wires cut across the backdrop of what looked to be ashen hills. I was photographing the backyard when a man rolled down his car window and said, "Can I help you?"

"This used to be her father's house," Genie said.

"In the 1950s," I explained.

"Come in for a tour," he said, and we followed him inside to the living room.

"You're standing where the old staircase began," the owner told me.

"What?"

"The original staircase," he said. "I moved it."

Jeanne had climbed the staircase to ask my dad—our dad—if she could go to the movies with her friends. I remembered my mom telling me that he'd lived on the top floor while his first wife and daughters had lived on the first floor.

The owner explained that the original staircase required you to ascend and descend in circles.

"Not a spiral staircase," he clarified. "It had hard angles."

He pointed at the new staircase.

I began to climb it.

I asked if the window had been there in 1961.

"The same window," he said.

It overlooked a string of houses. Was Jeanne a girl distracted by windows?

"Could you have looked out this window from the old staircase?" I asked.

"I think so," he said.

Did Jeanne pass the view and look? Not look?

I returned to the ghost of the staircase and tried not to look upset.

•

"How about we hit the cemetery?" Genie said.

"Sounds good," I said, staring out the car window at dilapidated houses set against a cloudless blue sky.

Genie told me about her town, something about the New York Yankees sending their laundry to Newburgh, something about White House dinner invitations, the Italian mafia. I tried to pay attention, but all I could think about was my resemblance to Jeanne. Did my dad see it?

"Here's where your father would have lived after Jeanne's death," Genie said, "right here across from the cemetery."

We pulled into the cemetery's drive and parked in section M. We split apart to search for the grave. I wanted to find it first.

Gravestones marched toward me from the horizon. I looked back at Genie. I had turned the search into an empty competition. What did it matter if I found it first? Jeanne, to me, was a concept. The real pull of her was my dad. I was trying to find my way back to him, I knew that. I walked through row after row, occasionally glancing back at Genie.

And then I found it: there, on the gray granite headstone, was an engraved image of the Virgin Mary. The Virgin's eyes looked down toward Jeanne's name, almost obscured by leaves.

But Jeanne was more than a name. She was a person, had been a person. She'd spent my whole life there, in the earth.

The shadow of two black maple trunks cut across the empty patch of land where my dad once planned to be buried.

I forgot to bring flowers.

The sun was too bright.

"I'm sorry," I whispered to the ground.

MENTAL ILLNESS

The next morning, I boarded the train back to New York City. I sat by a window, pulled out my notebook, and stared at a blank sheet of paper. I needed to make sense of the burial plot. I didn't know where to start.

The conductor asked for my ticket. I fumbled through my purse.

"Take your time," the conductor said.

The voice interrupted: *You're a failure*, and another voice added, *You should die*, and then together they repeated their words. Their whispers overlapped.

"I'm sorry," I said.

You lost the ticket, a voice said.

I lost my mind, I thought.

I apologized again and smiled.

"You have a beautiful smile," he said.

And then I remembered my mom telling me: "Your father said she was always smiling."

"Found it," I said, handing my ticket to the conductor.

He laughed.

"I want you to do something for me," he said. "I want you to relax."

•

"What are you doing?" Chris asked.

Surrounded by binders, color-coded folders, paper, highlighters, glue sticks, and pens, I was sitting on the floor, cutting out individual sentences from my manuscript. A week had passed since my visit to Newburgh.

"I'm gluing each sentence on its own piece of paper," I explained to Chris, "and then I'm freewriting based on that sentence as a way to deepen my work."

Each sentence about my dad brought memories with it, as if a roof had collapsed and I was trying to dig my way out.

I started shaking.

"I feel possessed," I said.

Chris tried to hug me. I shrugged him off.

"Jeannie's going to die," I said. "Jeannie's dead."

"What?"

•

"I keep losing control of my voice," I told my therapist. Two weeks had passed since my visit to Newburgh. "I keep saying 'Jeannie's going to die.'"

"Are you hearing voices?" he asked. "You can tell me."

"I don't have schizophrenia."

"Don't get hung up on names," he said.

"Me?"

"Let me call the hospital for you. You need the hospital. I spoke with your psychiatrist, and she agrees."

"I'll think about it," I said.

"I think—"

"I'll think about it," I insisted.

JEANNE

That evening I called my mom and asked her about Jeanne, if my dad had ever said anything more about her.

"When you were a little girl just learning to walk," she said, "our neighbor Sheila calls me at the hospital. I was still working there in medical records. Your father was at home with you. 'Barbara,' Sheila says. 'You better get home. Terry is pacing around the backyard, weeping and holding Jeannie. He won't put her down.' So I went home and gently asked your dad what was happening. 'It's just a hard day,' he said. That was in April or May. I took that to mean it was Jeanne's birthday. He was crying. You kept crying, but he refused to put you down. He was terrified you would hurt yourself."

After we hung up, I told Chris that I needed the hospital. I told him I liked the one in Westchester—the same hospital where I was taken three years ago after seeing Jeanne's photograph for the first time. I didn't make the connection aloud, but I thought it.

"It's a clean hospital. It's organized. It won't be convenient to visit," I told him, "but you don't have to visit."

"You know I'll visit."

"I won't be there for that long."

"Do you want me to take you?"

"I want to handle all this myself. It will make me feel sane."

I called the hospital, asked if they had any beds available in the ward for mood and personality disorders.

"Are you calling for yourself or someone else?" the receptionist asked.

"Myself, I guess."

MENTAL ILLNESS

The ward looked as I remembered it. The first long white hallway stopped at the nurses' station. Patients could turn right into the activities room or left into the second hallway. Patients couldn't enter the nurses' station. A nurse told me to sit outside the activities room while the staff searched my bags. A big whiteboard with the day's schedule—heavy on group therapy and name-your-emotion management (anger management, anxiety management, depression management, stress management)—and weather forecast (fifty-three degrees) faced me.

Last night, when I made the decision to admit myself, the hospital seemed purely abstract, but as I played with my hospital wristband and looked around, I registered the locked windows and locked doors. *Tell the doctors you made a mistake*, I thought. *Explain*

*the trip to Jeanne's grave, how any healthy person would have respond-
ed in the same way.* The wristband, I noticed, listed me as Barbara.

"Okay, Barbara," the nurse said, handing me back my bag.

I opened it.

"Where are my pens?" I said. "I need pens."

I tried explaining to her why I needed pens, that I was here
because I couldn't write and that without my pens I definitely
couldn't write.

"You can have pencils," she interrupted.

"I don't have pencils."

She disappeared into the nurses' station and returned with
two pencils.

"If you need more," she said, "just come find me."

I went into the activities room. The bookcase full of novels and old encyclopedias hadn't moved since my last stay, nor
had the long table in the far corner where arts-and-crafts time
was held on weekends. Two patients sat there piecing together a
thousand-piece puzzle. They each had a hard, determined look.

I sat at the window near a stack of board games. I burst out
laughing at their titles.

"Listen to this," I announced, and proceeded to read them
aloud: "Guess Who? Fact or Crap: It's Your Call! Would You
Rather? Taboo. Trouble. And, best of all," I said, "Guess Where?"

"You don't look like you belong here," one of the puzzle play-
ers said.

"But you sound like it," the other player said.

Then I went to the bookcase: *Whispers and Lies, Fragile, The
Geometry of Sisters, The Good Mother.*

My mom. I was afraid to tell her where I was.

EIGHTEEN

If I fail to bring my dad to life as a fully formed, unique character, my grief and his amount to nothing more than generic loss. Maybe I have a story filled with so much confusion and silence that it's impossible to render coherently.

When I stop writing, the anxiety returns. The calmness of writing comes from giving shape to experience. For example, when I describe my racing thoughts as "a flock of birds scattering from a field," I hopefully am describing racing thoughts in a way that no one else has.

Now I see a sequence of images—the playhouse he built in our backyard, the birdhouses he made for our backyard, the dollhouses that he made to look like our house. He never felt at home, he said, not until Ohio. He wanted to be buried in our backyard.

But my childhood house is no complete house; it's all broken up inside me: here the back porch, here the metal grate in my bedroom floor, here the wall between our bedrooms—each preserved, as a fragment, by itself.

MENTAL ILLNESS

"Is Barbara here?" a doctor asked those of us in the activities room.

"That's me," I said.

It was my second day in the hospital. I followed the doctor into the dining room and sat at a round table across from my "treatment team." The team consisted of my psychiatrist, my social worker, and two residents. My psychiatrist was the same psychiatrist I was assigned three years ago, the one who'd said: "You're a risk-taker, Barbara, and I can see you'll always be a risk-taker. You're not going to change."

This time, I asked to be called Jeannie.

"Why Jeannie?" the psychiatrist asked.

"I've always been called Jeannie. Spelled J-E-A-N-N-I-E."

I proceeded to explain that my parents had planned to name me Jeanne after a dead half sister.

"Without an *i*," I said.

I began to tell my treatment team about my recent visit to Jeanne's hometown.

"I stayed with a woman named Genie. G-E-N-I-E."

"You're manic," the psychiatrist alleged in a calm, impersonal tone.

"But my father died ten years ago. And he named me—"

"Your speech is pressured," he said.

"Of course my speech is pressured. I'm trying to condense my life into ten minutes."

I tried to tell him about my recent visit to my dad and Jeanne's hometown. I tried to explain why the trip overwhelmed me.

"Can you hear yourself?" he asked.

I thought: *I here'd myself, I can leave.*

MOM

Chris visited. We sat on a couch outside my room at the end of a long hall.

"Your mom called," he said. "I didn't answer. I didn't know what to say."

She and I talked on the phone almost every day, but the past month my calls home had been scattered.

"I worry about her worrying," I said.

"She can call me for support," he said, handing me his phone. "Please call her."

"We're not allowed to use cell phones," I said.

"No one's looking," he said. "Call her. Please. She's your mom."

I clicked "talk." It rang once.

"Hi, Mom."

"I've been so worried," she said.

"Everything is fine. Just having problems with my phone. I'm using Chris's cell."

Chris looked away.

"I've been so worried," she repeated.

230

"I'm fine. I promise."

A patient interrupted. He was new. He looked professorial.

"My name is John," he said. "My birth certificate is wrong."

"What's that?" my mom asked.

"Nothing," I said. "I'm outside on our stoop. It's just people walking by."

"Maybe they burned out my eyes," John said. "How could I have known? I was so young."

JEANNE

The hospital chaplain spoke with us about Jacob from the Bible. I had trouble focusing until she mentioned Jacob's renaming.

"And from then on he was Israel, literally 'he who struggles with God.' Can you think of an experience from your own life similar to Jacob's?"

I raised my hand.

"I was renamed," I said, and then I tried to explain the story behind my name. "And I recently visited Jeanne's grave."

"How did you feel after seeing her grave?" the chaplain asked.

"Pity for my father."

"But how did you feel? Sad, confused?"

"I don't know."

Someone else raised his hand. He said that five years ago, his older brother had died. His brother was eighteen, driving at night. There was a deer on an icy road. His brother swerved off the road and slammed into a tree.

"He didn't want to kill the deer," the patient said. "He was that kind of person."

The patient said that he filtered his life through his dead brother. "I devised a window system," he said, but became overwhelmed trying to explain. "I'm sorry. I'm not too good at finishing sentences."

After group, he and I talked. I asked him his age.

"Eighteen," he said as he looked out a locked window.

His brother was eighteen when he died.

MENTAL ILLNESS

I described few scenes in my journal from those few weeks in the hospital. I mostly charted my moods, temperature, and blood pressure. Writing felt harder than usual.

I made an erasure poem out of a newspaper, blacking out certain words. The ones left behind became the poem, but I don't remember what the poem said (I think there were "islands" and "desks"). Later my doctor asked if I thought the newspaper contained hidden messages for me to decode. A nurse must have found my poem, or maybe she just saw me blacking out words from the newspaper. In the context of a psychiatric hospital, any behavior can become a symptom.

MOM

For a decade I'd avoided, or tried to avoid, revealing my grief to my mom. With her grief, I didn't think there was any room for mine. So I forget exactly why I called her from the hospital phone. Chris had asked me to call her. My doctor had asked me to call her. But I'd been advised to call her during other hospitalizations.

So I don't think it was being told to call her that made me dial her number. I'd appear, appropriately, as "caller unknown."

"Hi, Mom."

I told her where I was.

"Do you think this has to do with writing?" she asked.

She sounded surprisingly calm. She knew that I was trying to write a book for my dad.

"No. Yes. Yes, but if not this, then something else would have brought me here," I said.

"I'm glad you're responsible," she said. "There's no shame in what you're doing. Do you want me to fly up there? I will."

"No, Mom, it's fine."

"Did my letter upset you?"

"Letter?"

"I sent you a letter. You've been asking me to write about my childhood. So I did. Well, I mostly wrote about meeting your dad."

"It must have arrived after I came here."

And then I told her about my visit to Newburgh.

"It was odd, being there," I said. "His grave next to hers is still empty."

"He never compared you with her. He adored you. You were the most perfect person to him."

How could he not compare me?

I compared everyone with him.

•

"I knew something was wrong," my mom tells me on the phone, bringing up the hospitalization. "I left a message with Chris. I told him he was going to be in big trouble if he didn't tell me what was wrong. I figured you were making him hide something from me."

"He kept telling me that I should tell you."

"He's a good guy. Your dad would have loved him." She pauses. "You can always tell me if something is bothering you."

"I know."

"When your dad didn't feel well, he wouldn't say anything. He didn't like to show weakness. It's not good to hold stuff in."

DAD

"My mom is visiting me in New York for Christmas," I reminded my psychiatrist. "Is there any way I can leave here this week?"

I'd been asking this question every few days for almost a month. I expected to hear another "possibly" or "we'll see."

"I think so," he said, which sounded more hopeful; I noted it in my journal.

But first, he said, another psychiatrist—"the leading expert on borderline personality disorder"—wanted to interview me.

"You definitely have a severe form of bipolar disorder," my psychiatrist said.

The question was whether I also had borderline personality disorder.

Grief seemed to me my primary diagnosis.

Jeanne seemed to me my secondary diagnosis.

But I agreed to review my story with another psychiatrist.

I sat at the head of a long table, in a private conference room. The borderline psychiatrist, a balding man with bright eyes and thin-rimmed glasses, sat to my left. About eight doctors, most of them young, also sat at the table and listened as I explained the history of my racing thoughts and hallucinations.

"The first time I experienced them, I must have been eleven or twelve. But back then I didn't think they were worth mentioning."

I talked about Jeanne, the house fire, and Genie.

"Any sane grieving person would question these coincidences, likely see them as signs. I think they are signs. If you think it's a delusion, that's fine."

"You keep mentioning that your father died ten years ago," the borderline psychiatrist said. "Why is this fact important?"

"The night before he died, I promised my dad I would write a book for him. I should have completed it by now."

Before I left the next day, my psychiatrist told me, "You don't have borderline."

I wanted him to say: *You don't have your dad. That's your illness.*

MOM

Chris borrowed a friend's car and picked me up from the hospital. As we drove back to our apartment, he kept reminding me how much he'd missed me. His eyes were red. He hadn't slept much, I could tell.

"I was miserable without you," he said. "At one point you told me that you thought you belonged in the hospital, that the other patients understood you."

I'd forgotten about that.

"I'm sorry," I said.

"I know it was harder for you than it was for me."

I didn't know if that was true.

As soon as I stepped into our apartment, I noticed a thick envelope on the kitchen table.

"It's from your mom," he said, and I hurriedly opened it.

•

My mom's letter sounds like she's sitting across from me, when really she wrote it six hundred miles away. It begins, "I'm going to start the story of when I met your Dad." "Dad" as opposed to "dad," "Dad" as opposed to "Father" or "father," he becomes at once casual and powerful, as he was in life.

"I know I'm making mistakes here," she writes. "I'm not a good writer." Yet her tall, black cursive looks confident, rarely tipping right or left. The stems of her *h*'s, *t*'s, and *l*'s touch the faint blue floor and ceiling of each ruled line.

"Believe it or not," she writes, "when I was in high school I used to write stories but was never encouraged to go anywhere with them."

My mom knows how to tell a story: "Terry's Dad died and he wanted to get married right away. He called the Judge, a gambling buddy of his, and asked if we could be married right away. He didn't want to travel to New York not being married. Terry was big on respect." For that brief moment he isn't my "dad" but rather the name on his gravestone. Maybe she wanted to avoid the hard alliteration of "Dad's Dad died." I doubt she intended to break the illusion he maintained: that his life began with me.

She wrote the letter, it seems, in one sitting, with at least two different black pens. On page twelve, the ink fades then darkens with "red geraniums." "He planted one hundred and fifty of them in our backyard," she writes. "Then he wanted birdhouses. The yard was full of them." I remembered now. I called him "Landlord of the Birds."

One memory leads to another memory, and another: "Finally he got his eye. He still rode the rides with you at Cedar Point. Every once in a while he would wake me up during the night because his eye fell out. We used to laugh."

In all thirty-one pages, only one word is crossed out: "me." She writes, "I know you believe in God and that's what keeps me going. I know I'm going to be with ~~me~~ him."

"Me" seems a fitting mistake. After he died, half of her followed him to wherever she believes he is.

"I talk with your Dad every night," she writes. "His T-shirt is under my pillow and I love him just as much. Isn't it sad that I can't remember truly being happy until I was 39 and marrying your father." There's no question mark.

•

My mom visited me in New York. My journal is mostly empty from that time. A sentence fragment here and there: "Nice to see Mom," "Writing, thinking, too difficult," "Need new medications, or need to stop taking these," "Attempting to keep it together for Mom," "Mom needs to believe I believe in God, so don't tell her I only believe when manic."

The longest entry from that visit: "My mom's hearing in her left ear is gone entirely. My dad's left vocal cord, then his left eye. What is it about the left of them? What will be left of me if I lose her?"

•

When I was a girl, my mom and I took long walks through town, and I'd listen to stories of a childhood so different from mine.

"I wouldn't wish how I was raised on my worst enemy," my mom tells me on the phone.

She mostly lived at her great-grandmother's house, a couple of blocks away from her parents' house. Well into her eighties, her great-grandmother cleaned houses for a living, and sometimes went away for entire weekends because of work. When that happened, my mom stayed at her parents' house. There, she slept with a steak knife underneath her pillow.

Late one night at her parents' house, when my mom was twelve, one of her mother's boyfriends woke her by pulling the sheets off her bed and told her, "My, my, my, someone is getting to be a big girl." My mom stabbed him in the shoulder with the knife. He ran out of the house, and when her mother learned what had happened, she beat my mom.

My mom had three siblings: Butch, Donna, and Eugene. "Eugene was so sweet," my mom says. "He'd give you the shirt off his back. But my mother, she was cruel, absolutely cruel to him. He had epilepsy and would get real bad seizures. He also was what they called 'tongue-tied' back then. He had trouble speaking. She actually told the neighbor children to call him a 'retard.' This one time, she held his arm against a burning-hot space heater. He was seven or eight. I think he took change out of her pocketbook to buy candy. It was awful, the burn marks on him. The old man"— my mom rarely calls him "dad" or "father"—"he didn't do anything about it. He knew. He just didn't do anything."

The last my mom heard, Donna was living in Indiana with her sixth—or maybe her seventh—husband. Donna and her children have been arrested "too many times to count," my mom says. A decade has passed since Butch showed up at my mom's back door, shouting and high on something. She didn't let him in because the local police had already warned her that he could be dangerous. Eugene died at thirty from a grand mal seizure.

"Why do you think you didn't end up like Butch or Donna?" I ask my mom.

"When I was a kid I'd go into the attic. It was a big attic," she says. "I'd sit there and write—make up stories, or play games by myself. I just hid. I had to get out. Our house was so filthy. You would not believe how filthy it was. Water bugs crawling out of the refrigerator. That's why I try to keep everything clean. And we didn't have locks on our doors. We lived across from the train depot and bums were always coming off the trains, trying to get into the house. I was often left alone. I had a dog to protect me. My mother, when she was home, which was rarely, had all these guys with her. The old man didn't care. He was living with his parents, and they took Butch. They didn't want me because I was a girl. Donna and Eugene weren't born yet. My great-grandmother was afraid something would happen to me with all those men around. She went to a judge by the name of Baxter. He told her to ask my parents if she could take me, and if they said no, he'd draw up the papers to grant her custody."

My mom's parents agreed to the arrangement.

"I adored my great-grandmother. She worked most of her life. Then, after I turned thirteen, her health got real bad. Doctors said she had 'a hardening of the arteries.' It was probably Alzheimer's.

She was starting to lose it. She moved in with my aunt and uncle. So I had to go back to my parents' house."

My mom wanted to join the navy after high school. She wanted to travel. Her father said no. So she perfected her typing skills and lined up a position as a secretary in Washington, DC. Her senior yearbook legend reads, "Has secretarial hopes."

"The old man scared me out of it," she says. "Told me how dangerous it was. 'You're going to get raped there,' he said. 'DC is so dangerous,' he said. He'd never been. But then he also told me that the day I graduated high school I was on my own. So he didn't want me in the navy, didn't want me in DC. I felt stuck. He was having a fit because I didn't want to get married. He said I'd be stupid not to get married."

My mom had been seeing a boy a few years older. He seemed nice enough, but not someone she wanted to spend the rest of her life with.

"The old man said, 'He doesn't drink. He doesn't smoke.' As if that mattered. A lot of good that did me. You know, the only time I can ever remember my mother giving me advice was on my wedding day. She said, 'You're making a mistake.' I wish I'd listened to her. I think I got married at six thirty at night. I don't think he and I were even talking that day. After the honeymoon, he changed real fast."

Sometimes he beat her until she turned black-and-blue.

"This one time my mother saw my bruises. She asked what happened. 'Oh nothing,' I told her. Well, she told the old man. He called me and asked, 'What'd you do to him?' My mother grabbed the phone from him and I hung up. The old man blamed me."

After my mom miscarried, her first husband invited his friends over to celebrate.

"I didn't have a happy life," my mom says, "until I met your father."

She wears my dad's wedding ring next to hers—to this day.

NINETEEN

Chris and I go out for lunch at a restaurant near our apartment and talk about writing.

"It'd actually be more experimental," I tell Chris, "to write a memoir that makes the author almost incidental, or invisible. So most things meta in memoir—a conversation like this one, for example—are pretty conventional. It's nothing more than hindsight perspective."

"Will you mention I have washboard abs?" Chris asks, taking a bite out of his burger.

"What?"

"If I'm in the book, give me washboard abs."

"I'm not going to deliberately lie about a minor physical detail."

"Come on."

"Okay. I'll figure out a way to say you have washboard abs."

DAD

A few weeks after my mom's visit, I stopped inside an antique store in my neighborhood. On the top shelf, next to a cameo glass lamp and a folded afghan, sat an anatomical model of the human eye. I reached for it.

"Here, let me help," a man said, and put it in my hands. "You can disassemble it and everything."

I lifted off the eye's upper hemisphere.

"I was talking to a customer the other day who was an eye doctor," the man said. "She said they still use these things in school."

"My father had an artificial eye," I said. "He could still cry from it on account of this part here, the lacrimal gland." I pointed to the flesh-colored piece sticking out of the upper hemisphere. "I think that's why, at least. I can't remember anymore. Is there a part missing? Something about it seems off."

"You just reminded me," he said. "Somebody was carrying it around the other day and dropped it."

He reached behind the shelf and picked the blue iris off the floor. I wanted it to be brown, like my dad's.

"I'll give it to you for seventy," the man said, "if you pay cash."

I agreed. I ran across the street, withdrew one hundred dollars from an ATM, and returned to find the eye wrapped in tissue paper and bagged.

I carried it to the nearby park and sat with it on my lap, my mind racing from *eye tissue* to *tissue paper* to *I need to write about my dad's eye on paper.*

MENTAL ILLNESS

A photograph of my dad and me hung on the living room wall in my apartment. In the undated photograph, we're kneeling on the grass. I'm in a white sundress. He wears a white dress shirt, slacks, and sunglasses. He's holding our mutt, Gigi. I look to be six or seven. The fence that he built—the fence that stretched across our driveway to protect me—is behind us. Behind the photograph was a decorative peacock feather.

"Did you put that there?" I asked Chris.

"What?" he said.

"The feather."

"You probably put it there and forgot," he said. "Why is it important?"

"The eye-spotted feather of the peacock tail, peacocks are male, my dad's eye. Don't you see?"

I searched the room. I turned over pillows. I wanted to find more feathers.

Chris was writing.

"What are you doing?" I said.

"I'm writing this down. It'll be useful for your therapist."

•

As I signed in at my therapist's office, I overheard a man say, "I think March 2."

I looked over. The two other men with him laughed.

"You think? You better know," one of them said.

I told my therapist, "That was a sign. Jeanne died on March 2."

I looked down at my notebook: "Tell therapist—cosmic coincidence."

"And today," I said, "a 'cosmic coincidence' was reported in the *New York Times*. Parts of a meteor fell into Siberia, and an asteroid is passing by Earth."

I looked down at my notebook: "Tell therapist—elephant whisperer."

I read aloud what I'd written: "The 'Elephant Whisperer' Lawrence Anthony died on March 2 last year. Two herds of South African elephants that Anthony rescued stood together near his house several nights after his death, according to his son. My last day at the hospital, a social worker distributed the story as part of an exercise. Anthony was sixty-two. My dad turned sixty-two the year I was born."

I looked down at my notebook: "Tell therapist—Genie/ Jeanne."

"And Genie, G-E-N-I-E, was a sign that I was getting closer to my half sister."

I handed him a typed letter by Chris, which explained the peacock feather incident, in addition to listing my symptoms, such as: "suddenly laughs without knowing why" and "assumes everyone hates her." According to the letter, I told Chris: "I feel overwhelmed . . . the world is giving each of us clues/symbols for us to find, we each have to find them. I'm finding my clues . . . the world isn't only offering clues to me. I'm feeling guilty that other people might not be seeing the clues meant for them."

My therapist looked at me, and in a kind voice said, "So what if they are signs? What then?"

I reminded him that Jeanne's childhood home caught fire the day before I interviewed her neighbor Bette. Also, the third floor caught fire—and that was the floor my dad lived on when Jeanne died.

"What if it's a coincidence?" my therapist said.

"How? I reached out to Bette, and the same day—that evening, actually—the house caught fire. Then the next day I learn all of it. And Bette wasn't in Newburgh. So it's not like she caused the fire."

"I didn't say—"

"I might be missing out on other signs," I said.

Afterward, I wandered through Manhattan with no destination in mind. I came upon St. Patrick's Cathedral, and I remembered learning that Jeanne had received her medal in this St. Patrick's.

I rushed into the church, sat in a pew, and opened my journal.

"Yes!" I wrote. "I'm in St. Patrick's where Jeanne received her medal. Everything is coming together: the third-floor fire—a sign to step back from my dad's life; Genie—a sign that a name is simply a name but that Jeanne is the focus of my story; 'the Elephant Whisperer,' like Jeanne, died on March 2—a reminder that grieving is a ritual."

•

My therapist, psychiatrist, friends—they advised me to put aside any writing about Jeanne or my dad.

"You don't understand this need," I told them. "It's a way to spend time with him."

But when I again worsened—crying at the supermarket, the ATM, the sight of a girl with someone resembling a father—I practiced not writing.

Not writing was worse.

I hit myself. I screamed at nothing.

Several months after my last visit I returned to the hospital, but this time, before admitting myself, I told my mom where I'd be.

•

I brought my "Mental Illness" binder with me to the hospital, and a young intern tried to take it away.

"I need it for school," I lied.

I explained that I was finishing graduate school for poetry, and was in graduate school for memoir: "I should have been done with the poetry program before the memoir one, but there was an administrative error on the poetry side, if that makes sense. It's too boring to explain."

She was in graduate school for psychology. Her thesis concerned the writing style and structure of patients with bipolar disorder and schizophrenia.

"Do you think the illness triggers the poetry or the poetry triggers the illness?" she asked.

"I don't know," I said. "Whatever I have makes whatever I write hard to write."

"Do you mind if I write that down?" she asked.

I told her she could.

Together we paged through my binder. We discussed a list of questions I had written: "Did I hide my illness from my mom because of bravery or guilt? Do I have an illness or is it grief? Do I have bipolar I disorder or schizoaffective disorder or borderline personality disorder? How does my dad see me?"

"Almost all of these are either/or questions," she said.

"How does my dad see me?" remains the crucial question.

"How" is an essential word.

Without "How," the question becomes: "Does my dad see me?"

•

The next morning, I met with the same doctor as before.

"I keep having these spasms," I told him. "My boyfriend had to restrain me."

"Restrain you?"

"I couldn't stop hitting myself. That's what he said. He writes down my behavior because I don't always remember."

"What about your writing?" the doctor asked. "Are you still writing about your father?"

"You told me to stop."

"Did you?"

I told him that I'd cut caffeine completely, slept between eight and nine hours every night, worked out every morning. I showed him my schedule ("I even schedule when I read the newspaper— I wait until the late afternoon because the stories make me cry").

"I really am trying to get better," I said.

"Are you still writing about your father?" he asked again.

"What counts as writing?"

"Have you written the words 'dad' or 'father'?"

"What if I write about him but call him something else?"

"What would you call him?"

"He loved birds. He built dozens of birdhouses. I could call him 'Landlord of the Birds.'"

"Try not to write," he said. "See what happens."

•

I dreamt my mom and I were inside a gutted house. She said she wanted to show me something. She tore off the living room carpet, and I realized we were in the room where my dad died. Suddenly I had a shovel and was digging. I hit something hard.

"Your poor father," she said, and I woke up.

My second night in the hospital, I dreamt my mom told me that my dad was still alive.

"What?" I said.

"Someone told me," she said. "That man down there."

And then I recognized my wood floors, my living room walls. We were in my apartment.

"Come on," I said, pulling her toward a window. "Don't trust that man."

I opened the window, but my mom was running away.

"He's a liar," I yelled, and I woke up.

The third night I dreamt my half sister Carol repeating, "I want nothing to do with you. I want nothing to do with you."

The fourth night I dreamt my dad was dying, and when I woke up I thought he was still dying.

The fifth night I dreamt I was leading him through my neighborhood, but he kept wandering off. I finally found him on a bodega floor, babbling to no one.

"Nightmares night after night," I told my psychiatrist. "Is it the medication?"

"I don't think so," he said. "I think it's grief."

•

Excited and relieved, I called Chris.

"My doctor here acknowledged my grief," I said. "He said I'm grieving."

The doctor's exact words: "You still have a severe form of bipolar disorder. It's complicated by a severe form of grief."

"Did he ever think you were not grieving?" Chris asked.

"None of my doctors ever focused on it. They really didn't ask about my dad. It was always, 'You have an illness.'"

TWENTY

I wish my doctors had acknowledged, did acknowledge, the illness as part of my grief, but they still maintain the grief is secondary. When I tell them that I hear voices or experience racing thoughts only when I remember that my dad isn't coming back—no matter how many pages I write about him, he's not coming back—the doctors remind me: "You have an illness." But as I near the end of *My Father's Glass Eye*, the illness looks like those distant ashen hills that Jeanne could have seen from her house in Newburgh. Had she lived long enough to lose our dad, would she have responded the way I did? Would she have blamed herself?

MENTAL ILLNESS

I stayed in the hospital for two weeks. My last day there, I reluctantly participated in another group therapy session. A new intern spoke to the patients slowly and loudly, as if we were deaf.

"Okay, everyone," she said. "Now please quiet down. We're going to do an exercise together."

The patient next to me whispered, "She'll get jaded soon."

The intern distributed a handout titled "Relationships Role Play" and read it aloud to us: "Consider a current relationship with someone close to you (spouse, friend, sibling, parent, child, etc.) with whom you are experiencing an obstacle. This may be a difference of opinion, difficulty communicating, or conflict over a particular subject. Choose a partner and describe the situation. Decide who will role play you and who will role play the person close to you. Then, role play a discussion where you address the issue in a calm way with the goal of reaching some understanding and/or resolution. Take turns with each partner's role play. This should take about 10–15 minutes per partner." She paired us off. I was assigned a patient my own age.

Meanwhile, a patient on the other side of the room raised his hand.

"The handout says that we can choose a partner," the patient said. "But you chose our partners. Also, 'role-play' should be hyphenated."

The intern ignored him.

My partner asked me to go first, so I briefly explained my situation.

"I'll be Arlene," the patient said.

"I'll be me," I said.

I didn't want to be me.

"I plan to write Arlene a letter," I said, "give her my number, and then she can call me if she's open to it. If I call her, it might be too intrusive. So let's pretend we're on the phone."

"Ring, ring," the patient said.

"Hello?"

"Jeannie, this is Arlene."

"Thank you so much for calling. I was hoping you'd call," I said.

"Why do you want to talk to me?"

"For a long time I've wanted to apologize for my name. I've often felt bad about it, that maybe my presence upset Carol and Debbie. You were understanding. You didn't blame me, or seem to blame me."

"I didn't blame you."

"There's another reason I called," I said. "I wanted to tell you this sooner. I started researching your sister Jeanne's life."

"What?"

"I visited your childhood home. I visited—"

"Why? Why didn't you tell me? You should've told me."

"I thought it'd upset you," I said.

"You should have told me," she repeated.

"I'm sorry," I said.

Chris appeared in the doorway. I was allowed to go.

JEANNE

I called my mom after being released from the hospital.

"I might contact Arlene," I told her.

"I think it's a good idea," she said. "You do share a father. And she always loved you."

For two months I labored over what to say. Should I explain my silence? Should I apologize?

And then on Father's Day, I wrote a simple letter to Arlene that said I missed her.

She called. Less than a week had passed since I mailed the letter. More than ten years had passed since we last spoke.

"You have to visit," she said. "Can you visit? You can't imagine how happy I was to see your name on the envelope."

•

Arlene lived less than an hour's drive away. Chris and I borrowed a friend's car, and he drove.

"I don't want to mention Jeanne," I told him in the car, "but it'd be dishonest not to mention her. I don't think I can tell Arlene the truth, that I've been researching her sister's life."

"Just see where the conversation takes you," he said.

Arlene was standing in her driveway when we arrived. She wore a fitted black-and-white dress and sunglasses. Her hair was still thick and dark. Her husband, Clyde, stood next to her.

She removed her sunglasses and hugged me.

"It's so wonderful to see you," she said.

I'd forgotten how much her eyes looked like our dad's.

We sat on their back porch overlooking a koi pond and talked. She reminisced about her visits to Ohio.

"Do you remember what you had in your bedroom when you were a kid?" she asked.

"A font of holy water?" I said.

"That's what I was thinking of," she said, and we both laughed. "Do you remember what you wanted to be?"

"A nun," I said, embarrassed.

"I think Chris is relieved you didn't go that direction," Clyde said.

"I don't think Dad was for that idea," she said. "I think it's for the best you didn't pursue it."

She asked me questions about my life in general.

"I write mostly," I said.

"What kind of writing?" Clyde asked.

"Essays, book reviews. Poems, I guess. That's what I studied in graduate school. But Chris is the poet. He's extremely talented."

I didn't say that I was writing a book for our dad.

"I remember when you left for college," Arlene said. "You were going to study journalism. Dad was so proud of you. You know, you're the only one of us to go to college."

"Did you ever want to go?" I asked.

"I did. I wanted to be a teacher. But I overheard Dad and my mom talking about money one evening when I was in high school, and I don't know. I thought that college must cost too much. So the next day I pretended that I didn't want to go."

"Do you still do journalism?" Clyde asked me.

"Not really. I mostly review other people's books," I said.

"Do you think you'll ever write your own?" he asked.

"You have more than enough material to write about," Arlene said.

This is your chance, I thought. *Tell her.*

"So," she said suddenly. "What's your penance?"

"Penance?" I said.

I didn't understand. I looked at Chris. He looked confused. Did she think I was punishing myself by visiting her? Did she know that I was researching her sister? I didn't ask her to clarify.

"For the longest time," I said, "I've felt bad about my name." I paused, thought: *Don't cry.* "I didn't learn about"—I didn't know how to refer to Jeanne—"my name, that I was named after your sister, until I was in the second grade." I could hear my voice shaking. "I've felt guilty ever since."

"It's nothing you should feel guilty about," Arlene said.

"Not at all," Clyde said.

She stood and said, "There's something I want to show you. Wait here."

"She's getting the album," Clyde said as she disappeared into the house. She returned with a photo album and handed it to me.

"You have to understand," she said, "our mother wanted nothing to do with us if we spoke to Dad. I couldn't put you in the main family album because of my mom."

"So you got your own special album," Clyde said.

I opened it, and noticed that almost every photo was of me. There were a couple of photos of our dad, but I found myself fixated on a photo of my mom and me—taken when I was in kindergarten. She was on the kitchen phone while I was on the orange rotary phone in the living room. Our relationship had developed into mostly that, I realized: her in Ohio, me in New York. Always on the phone.

At the end of the album were letters I'd sent Arlene and Clyde for various occasions, including Halloween. I wrote to them from a slumber party, reporting that I was learning how to write in "cursave."

Now I wanted to tell her that I was learning how to write about her sister.

"Dad couldn't talk about Jeanne," I told Arlene. "He kept her church medal. I don't know much about her."

Jeanne smiled a lot. She played with her sisters in their backyard. She received a medal from a church.

"She smoked," Arlene said. "She loved to smoke. She'd send me to the corner store to buy cigarettes. I wasn't even a teenager yet. 'Now here's some money for you to pick out your ice cream,' she'd say. She knew I loved chocolate ice cream."

And then, as Arlene started to talk about the car accident, her eyes searched the yard.

"The ambulance carrying Jeanne passed by Carol. Carol was in her car. She was on her way to show her baby to Jeanne, and here Carol didn't know—"

Clyde stopped her.

"Our mom blamed Dad," she continued. "I blamed him. We all did."

"For giving Jeanne permission to go out?" I asked as evenly as I could.

"Yes," she said.

We were both quiet for a moment.

"I don't know why Dad added the letter *i* to my name," I said. "Maybe—"

"Jeanne spelled her name with an *i*," Arlene said, "same as you."

The newspaper article about the car accident spelled her name *Jeanne*.

The yearbook spelled her name *Jeanne*.

My mom had told me that my dad chose to add the letter *i* to my name.

"I didn't know that," I said.

I looked down at the album open on my lap. There we were on the phone, my mom and me. The name no longer felt important.

MOM

A month after visiting Arlene, I boarded a train to Ohio—the same train that I rode the night before my dad died: 49 Lake Shore Limited. I drifted in and out of remembering my promise: I needed to finish a book for him.

My mom met me at the station in Sandusky.

"You must be tired," she said, hugging me. "Fifteen hours in that train. You should fly next time. It's worth the extra money. You know I'll pay."

On the short drive home, while she talked, I watched her hands on the steering wheel. The two wedding rings reminded me of how lucky I was. I was raised by parents who loved one another.

Once home, though, I found almost no trace of him. I felt like I was in a stranger's house—until I went upstairs. Framed photographs of him hung on her bedroom wall. There he was, in his work clothes at the hospital where he painted. There he was, in his pajamas with a cane—I wanted to throw it away. Why remember him like that?

I fell asleep, and in the morning, my mom said she wanted to go for a drive.

"Where?" I said.

"I don't know. I thought we could get out."

In the car, she asked about Chris and my friends in New York. I asked about her job at the library. We drove past cornfields and cows.

"Do you think you and Chris will stay in New York?" she asked.

"I don't know. I'd like for us to live near you."

And then I felt my throat narrowing. My thoughts raced too fast to catch. She'd turned onto the road to the cemetery.

"Do you want to visit Dad's grave?" she asked.

I looked out the window at a big empty field. I said nothing, could say nothing.

She started to say something and I interrupted, "Why would you suggest the cemetery? Why would you suggest that?"

"I just thought you might want to visit his grave. I thought that maybe you didn't want to ask."

"You can't just suggest something like that out of nowhere," I said.

I stared out the window, away from the cemetery, as we passed it.

"I'm sorry," she said.

No, I'm sorry, I didn't say.

I was being irrational, I didn't say.

I can't acknowledge Dad's gone, I didn't say.

She changed topics. I forget the topics.

We pulled into the driveway.

I went into the house while she fed some stray cats behind our garage. I decided to comb through photo albums and scrapbooks. I found handwritten letters from my dad that I hadn't read in a long time. In one, addressed to me when I was a baby, he described the most wonderful trip in his lifetime as a trip to the hospital to watch me being born: "I shall never experience a more beautiful trip. So you see when someone tells me of going on a trip, I always feel they will never have one as good as mine."

On the next letter, he'd sketched a portrait of me as a baby in a high chair crying, "I want my Daddy!"

I closed the album.

I went outside to find my mom. She was in the garage, in the back corner by the dollhouse that he'd built.

"I'm sorry," I told her.

"It's okay. It's not easy with him gone."

Inside the dollhouse were old unmarked VHS tapes, marbles, children's books. It hadn't been moved in probably twenty years. He'd made this dollhouse for me, but in some way it had also been for himself—proof that he could make something despite his eye, proof that he loved me.

"After I finish a book for Dad, I'm going to write a book for you."

"Don't do things for us," she said. "Do them for yourself."

TWENTY-ONE

For more than a decade I've used this book as an excuse to hold on to someone who can no longer be held. I've spent more time on the dead than the living.

My dad would not have wanted this.

"My dad would not have wanted . . ."

"He would have wanted . . ."

What do I want?

I want to stop missing him so much.

I want to stop writing this book.

I used Jeanne as a metaphor—as a means to understand my dad's grief, as a means to understand who he was, as a means to understand how I should grieve.

I don't know how to grieve.

Jeanne was a real girl.

I wanted to show why I loved him. I wanted to show how great he was. Yet how could I write a book about my dad, as private as he was?

"The less people know, the better," he often said, "It's nobody's business," "You can't trust nobody."

So I revealed more than I wanted to reveal about myself—as if losing my mind after he died proved how great he was.

"You can't call me perfect," he often said. "Nobody's perfect," "You have to let yourself make mistakes," "You're perfect," "I'm proud of you no matter what."

No matter what?

I left, and he died.

Did I think a book would bring him back?

And what did I expect to do with it anyway? Sit at his grave and read it to the dirt?

"I can't kill myself," I told myself every time I wanted to kill myself. "I haven't finished a book for my dad."

I've since found in old journals different versions of my promise: "I'm going to write a book for you, so everyone knows how much I love you." "I'm going to write a book for you, so everyone knows how great you are."

Which is it then? Did I promise to prove his greatness? Did I promise to prove my love?

What were the last words he heard me say?

"Dad" was my first word.

JEANNE

A few months later I was in McCarren Park with my friend Stephanie. The park separates our two neighborhoods.

"I don't think I'll ever finish the book," I told her.

"But you have," she said. "I read it."

"No, that doesn't count."

"Why?"

"My professor said readers of memoir need to know that you—the writer—are okay by the end. But I don't know if I'll ever be okay. I'll always miss my dad. I still cry about him, and he died more than a decade ago."

"Wait—Jeannie, do you see that?"

"What?"

"That guy, he's wearing a shirt that says 'Jeannie' on it—spelled how you spell it."

"Oh, weird."

"I wonder what it's about," Stephanie said. "There's a picture of a woman on the shirt."

We continued walking. I told her that I'd decided to return to the memoir MFA program, after taking a break because of the hospitalizations.

"Turns out," I mentioned, "one of my future classmates is named Jeanne. Well, I don't know if she pronounces it *Jean* or

Jeannie. I hope it won't be weird for her to be in class with me—given what I'm writing about."

"Weird for her?" Stephanie asked.

"I'm fine with it," I told her. "It's not weird for me."

We reached Stephanie's apartment, and she invited me upstairs.

"No, I should get home. I have so much writing left to do."

As I made my way home, I passed a circle of people wearing shirts that read "Jeannie." They were holding balloons.

"One!" they shouted. "Two! Three! Jeannie!"

They let the balloons go and started singing "Happy Birthday." On their shirts was a picture of a young woman. Years were listed underneath it. A dash separated the years. Some of the people were crying.

●

Chris was home early from work. We fixed dinner together, took a walk. He suggested the park.

"There was a birthday party here today," I told him, "apparently for a dead girl named Jeannie—spelled the same as my name. A bunch of people wore shirts that said 'Jeannie.'"

"Really?"

"Yeah. Her picture was on the shirts. She looked young, in her twenties maybe. And when I passed the people, they all shouted, 'One, two, three, Jeannie,' then let go of balloons and sang 'Happy Birthday.'"

"That's so strange. Are you going to write about it?" he asked.

HOME

The dollhouse my dad made needs repainting. The windows need new screens. The wallpaper could be replaced. The carpeting should be cleaned. The roof has started to fade.

I try to remember how we arranged the rooms. The staircase always stayed where it was, underneath a hole between the first and second floors. The kitchen went on the first floor because that's where my dad installed the linoleum. The second and third floors he carpeted.

"Where should the living room go?" I asked him.

"If we put an area rug on the first floor," he told me, "the living room could go off the kitchen."

So he made an area rug. The second floor became the daughter's bedroom. The top floor is where her parents slept. But usually the parents and the daughter stayed together on the first floor.

Lifting off the roof revealed the attic where the daughter stored her toys, but I pretended she was too mature for those.

The dollhouse was about pretending.

This book is about pretending.

I pretended he watched me write it.

I'm pretending he'll someday read it.

•

A couple years later, just as I'm finishing this book, a job brings me to Baltimore. I've been hired to teach college students how to write about their lives. Chris moves with me, and we rent an uneven row house with two floors, front and back porches, a basement, a dining room. Even a yard. Most importantly, each of us has our own office. Sure, our desk chairs roll to the left if left alone. I block mine with a bookend shaped like a monkey. Chris uses a thick green shag rug to park his chair. We slip ceramic coasters underneath one side of the cat tree. We feel lucky.

•

Surrounded by stacks of flap-lock moving boxes, I want to finish unpacking but Chris insists we take a break.

"We've already been here two weeks," I tell him.

"We've only been here two weeks," he says. "Let's get some food."

We walk to the organic grocery store across the street. We put frivolous things in our cart: kalamata olive hummus, chips made of lentils, kombucha. We don't feel brave enough to try the honey-mustard dried crickets.

"We're ridiculous," I tell him as we get in the checkout line.

A sign lists the products the store refuses to sell. My favorite sriracha is banned. Something about a preservative. It's that sort of neighborhood: record stores, bookstores, cafés, a curiosity shop that sells small raccoon-skull planters and century-old morphine prescriptions.

"I have an idea," I tell him while we wait in line. "What if we buy a duplex, or some house broken into two apartments? I could use the money my parents saved for me for college. It'd cover a down payment—probably not in this neighborhood, but that's ok. My mom could live in the house with us, but she'd have a separate entrance, her own space. It's the only way she can afford to move here. If I frame it as an investment for me, then she might go for it."

"It'd be nice to have your mom close," he says.

"She'd be really close."

"I love your mom," he says. "Of course I'm ok with it."

•

Inside one of the moving boxes marked SENTIMENTAL is a wood box my dad made. It holds our Cedar Point season passes from the 1980s and '90s. There's also a newsletter from Providence Hospital, dated the year I was born. It reads: "CONGRATULA-TIONS TO TERRY VANASCO, head painter of the maintenance department, our EMPLOYEE OF THE MONTH." I also find a card I made for him when I was a child. I used blue checkered wallpaper for the front and back. I drew a brown tree and a yellow sun. On one of the branches I wrote: "Happy Father's Day!!" The message inside: "Dear Dad, I love you and want to thank you for everything you have done for me." The wallpaper is the same wallpaper he used for the dollhouse kitchen.

I open another box, this one full of Chris's family photos. I get his toolbox. I need nails.

While Chris is out running errands, I hang our family photos on the wall along the stairs. After hanging a few, I stand back. They're uneven, but I know Chris won't mind.

When he comes home, he helps me finish.

ACKNOWLEDGMENTS

Masie Cochran, my editor, is the reason *My Father's Glass Eye* finally exists. I would still be manically revising my manuscript if not for her enthusiasm, questions, instincts, trust, and brilliance. Diane Chonette, the Tin House art director, made my memoir look beautiful, inside and out. I hope people judge my book by its cover. Tremendous gratitude as well to Nanci McCloskey, Sabrina Wise, and the whole phenomenal team at Tin House. Also, special thanks to Anne Horowitz and Allison Dubinsky, whose thorough copyediting and proofreading revealed mistakes and new meanings. And gratitude to Victoria Marini, my agent, for leading *My Father's Glass Eye* to Tin House.

Portions of *My Father's Glass Eye* have appeared in another form in the *Believer*. Without the *Believer*, my personal writing might never have found readers beyond professors, classmates, and friends. The magazine's editors, past and present—especially Karolina Waclawiak, Andi Winnette, Hayden Bennett, and Ed Park—possess supernatural powers with words.

Alexandra Styron's tireless dedication, generosity, and Job-level patience—long after I graduated from Hunter—will never be forgotten. Kathryn Harrison, Meena Alexander, Louise DeSalvo, and my genius Hunter comrades and friends—Molly Englund, Kate Neuman, Alice Neiley, Jeanne Hodesh, and Amy Jo Burns—gave crucial feedback and reassurance. Hunter College and New York University's MFA writing programs offered time and support, and Poets House gave me a quiet place to write.

I am forever deeply indebted to Meaghan Winter, Stephanie Palumbo, and Anita Anburajan. They read countless drafts over several years, and I never had to ask. I also want to acknowledge Stephanie's grandmother, Erna Trocola. Her stories are inspiring and important, and I hope Stephanie keeps telling them.

Special thanks to Sally Leaf, Leigh-Anne Goins, Jenna Kahn, Adam Germinsky, Courtney Allison, Rachel Riederer, Kevin Mulligan, Loren Lynch, and Madeleine Kuhns for listening to me talk about the book.

Genie Abrams and Bette Jefferson helped with difficult research, and I am deeply grateful to them.

My Northwestern professors—especially John Keene, Mary Kinzie, Reg Gibbons, Brian Bouldrey, and Robyn Schiff—taught me how to construct emotions with words. They made writing possible.

For sharing their poems, stories, and essays with me, tremendous gratitude to all my students.

And finally, my family—those I included and those I didn't.

Chris's love has given me a happy ending, and my love for him will never end. He has improved my life in ways too profound to describe.

My love for my mom is indescribable and unquantifiable. She insisted that I write anything I wanted, or anything the book needed. I could not have written this without her encouragement, understanding, and love. Every day I feel like the most loved daughter in the world.

I did this for my dad—even though he will never know. He always kept his word. I tried to keep mine.

Also by the author

How can even the 'nice guys' do terrible things to us? Fifteen years ago, Jeannie's relationship with a close friend ended in rape. With the rise of the #MeToo movement, recurring nightmares of the event that plagued her as a girl have returned. To process her conflicted feelings she resolves to face her trauma head-on.

Through transcribed interviews with the perpetrator and discussions with the women closest to Jeannie, her compelling memoir explores how the incident impacted both of their lives, while examining the culture and language surrounding sexual assault and rape. *Things We Didn't Talk About When I Was a Girl* is a necessary book for our times and a springboard for other women to share their stories.

Things We Didn't Talk About When I Was A Girl;
9780715653753; £9.99

MELISSA FEBOS: 'Exactly the book we need right now. Vanasco's honesty and willingness to interrogate both her rapist and herself enthralled me. I wish everyone in this country would read it.'

DANIEL GUMBINER: 'In a moment where morality is so often rendered in flat, simplistic terms, Vanasco refuses to take the easy way out: she is generous yet exacting, fair yet relentless. A searching, brilliant book.'

ANGELA PELSTER: 'Vanasco's wildly courageous decision to confront her rapist, question him, meet with him, and then invite her readers into her processing of that experience is, frankly, stunning.'

YZ CHIN: 'Explores the common experience of rape with uncommon nuance and intense tenderness.'

LISA LOCASCIO: 'Jeannie Vanasco's rigorous and nuanced investigation of crime, trauma, secrets, and the telling of our stories applies an agile mind and penetrating insight to the enforced silences that surround rape and its aftermath.'

KRYSTAL A . SITAL: 'Wickedly clever and powerful... a necessary book.'

TIM TARANTO: 'Interrogates the terms of betrayal, the limits of redemption, asking us how can we forgive when we never truly forget?'

AMY JO BURNS: 'Vanasco cuts through the silence of deep betrayal, gives contour to the aching space between forgiveness and absolution, and offers a living testament to the endless wreckage of sexual assault.'

EMILY GEMINDER: 'Extraordinary. This is a brilliant book, an astonishingly fierce inquiry into the places language won't go.'

THOMAS MIRA Y LOPEZ: 'A work of astounding control, able to reach places I never expected a book to reach. It left me transfixed.'